# Air Capabilities of the U.S. Navy SEALs

# Air Capabilities of the U.S. Navy SEALs

## A HISTORY OF BRAVERY AND INNOVATION

By
Norman H. Olson
Captain (SEAL) USN, Retired
and
Commander (SEAL) Tom Hawkins, USN, Retired

*Air Capabilities of the U.S. Navy SEALs*
www.PhocaPress.com/air-capabilities
Copyright © 2017 by Norman Olson and Tom Hawkins

Layout and design by Lisa Merriam
Cover design by Bob Wood

Published by Phoca Press
New York, NY 10025
www.PhocaPress.com

ISBN-13: 978-0-9909153-5-5

10 9 8 7 6 5 4 3 2

# Contents

# ACKNOWLEGEMENTS

This book would not have been possible without the assistance of my good friend and fellow SEAL Teammate Tom Hawkins. Some months after working on the book, I experienced an unexpected stroke, which took away, among other things, my ability to work as I once did on the computer. Tom came to the rescue and assisted me in every way. He was an exceptional SEAL officer with a diversified career that involved research, development, the test and evaluation of new and improved operational equipment; and planning, programming, budgeting, and development of doctrine surrounding many aspects of Naval Special Warfare. Like me, and often with me, he was involved in many of the actions, activities, and decisions made during the early growth of the Naval Special Warfare community. His background, experience, and support were invaluable.

Lisa Merriam's work and support were priceless. She devoted untold personal time, computer time, and travel time recording and transcribing interviews and laying out many versions of the manuscript that finally became the book. I especially thank her for tolerating my ranting and raving, which have become my trademarks, a.k.a. "Stormin' Norman." I know she secretly loves it. She kept me on course when I was ready to throw in the towel. Her superb technical skills and patience reminded me that all books published ultimately come from a team effort.

Thanks also to some of my crusty old friends and SEAL operators who provided personal insights and assisted in jogging my memory in many ways. Foremost were Bill Bruhmuller, Lenny Waugh, Frank Moncrief, Pierre Ponson, Ty Zellers, and Jim McGee99 and Gene Gagliardi: both deceased; men of great skill and daring. These men were true pioneers in many of the capabilities discussed in the book. Sadly, Bill Bruhmuller passed away unexpectedly as we were preparing this book, but his memory, as well as those of Jim and Gene, will live on through their many contributions.

No worthy book can make it to press without the help of others. In particular I'd like to acknowledge Liz Logan with the National Navy UDT-SEAL Museum for researching and providing several rare photographs.

Thanks also to Jim Woods of the Navy Parachute Team for dramatic and vivid photographs of today's Leap Frogs in action, which, in many ways, provide insight to the vast tactical parachuting capabilities of the modern SEAL Teams. Special thanks to Rich Graham of Trident Fitness Tactical in Tampa for the rappelling images. I am indebted to Chris Bent for spectacular historic photographs of his spacecraft recoveries and to Mike Mallory for the Apollo 11 images.

This book, my life, and my career could not have been accomplished without the love, support, and sacrifices of my wife Bobbie. The job of a Navy SEAL wife is as a tough one. Because of the demanding, unpredictable and clandestine nature of our work, SEAL husbands need highly adaptable and independent wives. There was so much time we couldn't spend together, so many experiences we couldn't share, so many responsibilities I couldn't help shoulder. I am just so grateful that despite all that, Bobbie still chose to share her life with me. That this beautiful, talented, and accomplished woman has been willing to put up with Naval Special Warfare and this particular operator is one of the greatest blessings of my life.

# PREFACE

Under the cover of darnkess on the night of 25 January 2012, a classified number of U.S. Navy SEALs jumped into the abyss of the sky at a very high altitude from the tail ramp of a U.S. Air Force Special Operations Command C-130 aircraft. After in-air maneuvers, they landed by parachute into East Africa some 12 miles from the Somali town of Adow. Upon landing, they rallied on the ground, and patrolled to a remote and barren region known to be where Jessica Buchanan, an American citizen, and Poul Hagen Thisted, a Danish citizen, were being held by Somali pirates for $1.5 million ransom. The SEALs engaged and eliminated nine pirates, thus, completing a successful hostage-rescue mission. The details of the mission itself remain classified; however, elements are discussed in the book *Impossible Odds*, written by Jessica Buchanan and others. This mission resulted in the application of tactical parachuting not accomplished anywhere else in the world.

The "Trident" Navy SEAL breast insignia includes an anchor to represent the Navy, a trident to represent the sea, a pistol to represent land, and an eagle to represent the air—the three environments in which Navy SEALs operate. This book provides a history of "Air" capabilities now resident in Naval Special Warfare, where Navy SEALs are masters, and how they evolved.

Air capabilities within today's SEAL Teams include parachuting, use of helicopters, and fixed-wing aircraft. It is parachuting, however, that most people think of first, and parachuting was indeed one of the earliest air capabilities developed by the SEALs.

During World War I, observation balloon pilots were issued parachutes as rescue devices in case they had to bail out. During World War II, U.S. Marine Corps and U.S. Army troops were trained in parachuting; however, the only parachuting operations conducted were by the Airborne Divisions of the U.S. Army. Parachutes were also employed by the Office of Strategic Services (OSS), which was a U.S. intelligence agency formed during World War II to coordinate information gathering, espionage, sabotage, and subversion behind enemy lines.

It was only after World War II that skydiving became a hobby when excess military parachutes were used to begin freefalling for sport. Parachuting was introduced to the Underwater Demolition Teams (UDTs) in the early 1950s. Though it was an alien concept to the older frogmen, it was of great interest to the younger Team members that volunteered in mass when the first opportunity presented itself to attend the Army's Basic Airborne Course at Fort Benning, Georgia. These early pioneering efforts significantly enhanced the current tactical parachute capability mastered by today's SEALs.

Most people today don't realize that the first Navy SEAL Teams were culled from the Navy's famed UDTs that were first organized during World War II. The UDTs were tasked to accomplish intelligence collection through hydrographic reconnaissance and, as necessary, demolition of natural and man-made obstacles preceding amphibious landings. The UDTs remained doctrinally organized after the war within the Amphibious Force, and set out to expand and improve the scope of their operational capabilities.

It was during the post-war period that the UDTs adopted many of the underwater capabilities of the OSS Maritime Unit (OSS MU). It did not include the significant OSS parachuting capabilities, which were never employed by OSS MU. Incorporating OSS methods displayed the UDTs interest in improving their overall tactical operational capabilities. Parachuting was eventually adopted by the UDTs, and these capabilities progressed into the SEAL Teams.

Of the "within the Air" capabilities of our Navy SEALs, the evolution of tactical parachuting is the primary focus of this history. The high-altitude parachute insertion to rescue Jessica Buchanan and Poul Thisted didn't just happen. Parachuting capabilities didn't start in the UDT and SEAL Teams, but it was in these maritime special operations units that the tactics and techniques of parachuting have evolved, often through trial and error, and now stand as arguably the foremost air assault operational capabilities in the U.S. military.

The UDTs never parachuted tactically during World War II or during the post-war period. It was not until the Korean War era that they seriously began investigating and implementing capabilities for parachuting. The SEAL Teams expanded, enhanced, and refined all of the air capabilities that they employ today. And many tactical air operations do not involve parachuting at all. The story here will be as comprehensive as possible, however, little formal documentation exists regarding development of many of the air capabilities attempted or actually implemented within the SEAL Teams. With the help of others, I have gathered rare, first-hand accounts by several of the frogmen involved. Today, parachuting is a standing mission-essential task for all SEAL operators, and all SEALs are qualified in freefall parachuting. SEALs employ two parachuting capabilities: High-Altitude, Low-Opening (HALO) and High-Altitude, High-Opening (HAHO), where each has tactical advantages.

The story also involves the use and evolution of helicopters and fixed-wing aircraft to conduct parachuting and a variety of other maritime special operations capabilities; including the little-known role UDT and SEAL operators played in support of America's space-flight program.

While I was not among the first parachutists in the UDT-SEAL Teams, it was my good fortune to be involved in much of the early freefall parachuting development and refinement. The "Air" story of the UDT and SEAL Teams is robust, fascinating, exciting, and accomplished by men of great bravery and skill.

Captain (SEAL) Norman H. Olson, USN, Retired.

11

# CHAPTER 1

# EARLY UDT AIR CONCEPTS

In his book, *The Naked Warriors,* first released in 1956, the instrumental UDT commanding officer Commander Francis Douglas "Red Dog" Fane wrote the first definitive accounting of the UDTs from their establishment during World War II through the Korean War period. In this book, Fane never discusses air experimentation or capabilities, yet, in the late 1940s and early 1950s, UDT-2 and UDT-4, the operational units under his command at the Naval Amphibious Base, Little Creek, Virginia, experimented with helicopters as a means of recovering men from the water. While no documentation of these events has been discovered, photographs were taken and provide a visual record.

A U.S. Navy Sikorsky S-51 helicopter winches in a UDT operator off the beaches of the Naval Amphibious Base, Little Creek, Virginia, circa, 1947.

During this period, helicopters were relatively new to the military inventory, and didn't have the space and lift capacity with which to develop any kind of true UDT operational capability.

There is no record of UDT men entering the water from helicopters during this period; only using the helicopters winching system to haul them in. While experimental, the helicopter back then was most likely seen as a method for enacting the emergency rescue of a UDT operator in peril. What is most important is that the UDT men were always seeking better tactics, techniques, and procedures to enhance or expand their air and other operational capabilities. It was only after the Korean War that serious operations with parachuting and helicopters began in earnest within the UDTs.

# CHAPTER 2

# PARACHUTING:
# AN HISTORICAL PERSPECTIVE

Before delving into the specifics of the UDT and SEAL Team parachuting and other air capabilities, an historical perspective about parachuting and its development within Naval Special Warfare is warranted.

The first written account of a parachute concept can be found in Leonardo da Vinci's notebooks (circa 1495). The sketch he drew consisted of a cloth material pulled tightly over a rigid pyramidal structure. Although Da Vinci never made such a device, he is given foremost credit for the concept of lowering man to the earth safely using a maximum drag decelerator.

In 1797, the Frenchman Andrew Garnerin made the first jump with a parachute without a rigid frame. One of Garnerin's balloon jumps from 8,000 feet, a very high altitude for the time, was observed by the French astronomer Jerome Lalandes. As the parachute descended, severe oscillations were induced in the canopy. Lalandes suggested cutting a small hole near the apex of the canopy to inhibit the oscillations. This modification, now known as the vent, did dramatically reduce canopy oscillations as Lalandes had suggested.

During the next century parachuting was confined to carnivals and daredevil acts. Acrobats would perform

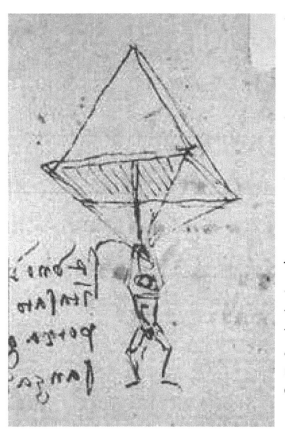

Sketch from Da Vinci's notebook.

14

Illustration of the death of Robert Cocking in 1837.

Thomas Baldwin was a pioneer balloonist and Army Major during World War II. He was the first American to descend from a balloon by parachute.

stunts on a trapeze bar suspended from a descending parachute. The parachute was released from a hot-air balloon by attaching the top of the parachute to the equator of the balloon with a cord that broke after a person jumped from the basket (more or less like static-line parachuting today). Public opinion became very unfavorable towards the use of parachutes when the Englishman Robert Cocking fell to his death in 1837. Cocking jumped an inverted cone-shaped parachute (point down) from 5,000 feet and was historically distinguished by becoming first parachuting fatality.

The next major contribution to parachute systems was development of a harness by Captain Thomas Baldwin in 1887, a pioneer balloonist, who served as a Major in the U.S. Army during World War I. Baldwin was wearing a rope-harness attached to a folded silk arched-canopy, which was collapsed and stowed in a canvas container attached to the side of a balloon basket. He jumped from an altitude of 5,000 feet and landed safely. Baldwin also designed this first frameless parachute for his circus act, which was opened by the wind after the jumper's body-weight pulled it free from the balloon, and air pressure kept the canopy deployed.

Kathchen Paulus preparing to jump.

Kathchen Paulus poses on a ticket to one of her events.

The concept of folding or packing the parachute in a knapsack-like container was developed by Paul Letteman and Kathchen Paulus in 1890. Katchen Paulus was a rare female professional parachute jumper in aerial exhibition shows from the late 1880's to the early 1900's.

Their canopy apex was tied to the interior of a canvas bag, and the lines and canopy were folded inside. The canvas bag was closed with a break cord attached to the balloon for ascent. As the jumper fell away from the balloon, the cord would break and release the stowed parachute. Katchen Paulus also demonstrated the first intentional breakaway – an action after a first parachute was inflated, released, and a second parachute was deployed.

In 1907 Charles Broadwick demonstrated two key advances in the parachute he used to jump from hot air balloons. He folded his parachute into a pack that he wore on his back, and the parachute was pulled from the pack by a static line attached to the balloon. When Broadwick jumped from the balloon, the static line became taut, pulled the parachute from the pack, and then snapped.

Jumping in San Diego in 1914, Charles Broadwick hoped to persuade the U.S. Army to adopt his "coatpack" for military aviators' safety, which they did.

Charles Broadwick in 1915.

With the start of World War I, Broadwick saw great potential for his coatpack parachute or "life preserver of the air." In 1914 and 1915, the parachute was demonstrated to congressmen, the United States Army, and pilots. The Army purchased two packs for testing, but didn't evaluate them until after the war.

The military still didn't believe that the human body could tolerate the experience of freefall for more than a few seconds before "blacking out." Skeptics were convinced in 1919 by Leslie Irvin and Floyd Smith. They demonstrated freefall jumps and developed the ripcord at the parachute testing and training center at Wright Field (now Wright–Patterson Air Force Base) in Dayton, Ohio, which was established in May 1917 by the U.S. Army Air Service during World War I.

On 1 March 1912, U.S. Army Captain Albert Berry was the first in the United States to jump from a fixed-wing aircraft while flying above Jefferson Barracks, St. Louis, Missouri. The 36-foot diameter parachute was contained in a metal canister attached to the underside of the plane—when Berry dropped from the plane, his weight pulled the parachute from the canister. Rather than being attached to the parachute by a harness, Berry was seated on a trapeze bar. According to Berry, he dropped 400 feet before the parachute opened. Credit for the first U.S. jump has also been claimed by Grand Morton, who made his jump on 28 April 1912.

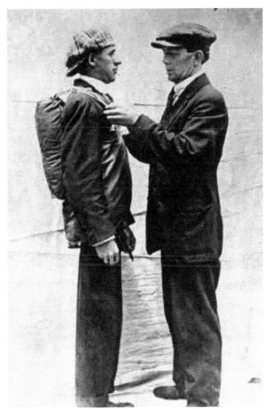

Charles Broadwick adjusts the fit of a coat-pack on an unidentified aviator. His simple and ingenious invention continues to assist parachutist today. Virtually all parachutes are now stowed in packs that are strapped to a jumpers back.

Wilber Wright Field and Fairfield Air Depot, Dayton, Ohio, circa 1920.

Charles Broadwick in 1915, around the time of more demonstration jumps for the U.S. Army.

# TINY BROADWICK

## THE FIRST LADY OF PARACHUTING

**Born: April 8, 1893 Died: 1979**

In 1908, 15-year old Georgia "Tiny" Jacobs witnessed Charles Broadwick performing in an exposition and decided that's what she wanted to do. She approach Broadwick and, after some convincing, Tiny was added to the touring show, where she became an instant headliner. She subsequently adopted the name Tiny Broadwick, and went on to become famous for her numerous parachute jumps, many of which were "firsts" in every category. Tiny made her first jump in 1908 at age 15.

Georgia "Tiny" Broadwick as a young girl.

Most of Tiny's jumps were with aerial barnstorming shows. Tiny was billed as "The Doll Girl," a name she hated with a passion. She wore a silk dress and ruffled bloomers while jumping. Tiny broke bones, dislocated a shoulder, landed in swamps, was dragged by her parachute, and leaped from a burning balloon with barely enough altitude to open her parachute. She kept great enthusiasm no matter what the adventure.

Tiny prior to jumping in a barnstorming show.

Tiny Broadwick and Glenn Martin in 1913.

Tiny back on the ground.

In the early barnstorming days, jumpers sat on a trapeze type swing attached to flat circular silk parachutes. You literally were at the mercy of the wind. Her perspective was: "If you landed in a tree you were all right, but if you landed on a rooftop and rolled off, you were hurting."

In 1912 on a field south of downtown Los Angeles, Tiny ascended with a hot-air balloon and did a double parachute drop; descending partway with one parachute, then cut it away to open a second parachute to complete her spectacular jump. Observing this jump was businessman Glenn Martin, who later manufactured airplanes. Martin enrolled Tiny as his company's demonstrator. In June 1913, he dropped Tiny from his biplane over Griffith Park in Los Angeles, and two months later, he dropped her from a hydroplane over Lake Michigan. Wearing Charles Broadwick's coatpack, she became the first woman to parachute from an airplane and the first person to parachute from a hydroplane. Not only was Tiny the first woman to make an airplane jump; she was also the first woman to also make a freefall jump. She subsequently completed over 1,100 jumps.

"I was never afraid. I'd go up any time, any place. The only thing I hated was getting back to earth so quickly," she said.

Tiny preparing to jump.

# CHAPTER 3

# AIRBORNE MILITARY FORCES

Creation of airborne units had been proposed during World War I to assault behind the German lines in 1917. The first modern operation considered was in late 1918, when U.S. Army Major Lewis Brereton and his commander, Brigadier General William "Billy" C. Mitchell, suggested dropping elements of the U.S. 1st Division behind German lines near Metz in France. General Mitchell was convinced that U.S. troops could be rapidly trained to drop from converted bombers to land behind Metz in synchronization with a planned infantry offensive. The operation was planned for February 1919, however, the war ended before such an attack could be seriously planned. Following the war, the U.S. Army continued to experiment with the concept of having troops conducting airborne operations.

From World War I to the early 1930's, solid cloth parachutes remained unchanged in structure. They were used primarily by military forces in Europe, Russia, and the United States. The first true mass-paratroop drop was actually accomplished by the Italian military during experimentation with the Salvatore parachute in November 1927. The Salvatore was harnessed to the jumpers back and deployed with a static line attached to the drop aircraft. The method proved relatively quick and reliable, making it possible to jump from much lower altitudes. This is the same method used by U.S. Army airborne troops in the modern day. Within a few years, several battalions had been raised by Italy, and eventually formed into two airborne divisions. Although these two divisions would later fight with distinction in World War II, they were never used in a parachute drop.

During the inter-war period, development and experimentation with parachute troops was patchy. Britain, France, and the United States ignored the concept, while Russia, Italy, and Poland readily accepted the idea. In the Soviet Union, parachuting became a national sport with thousands of Russians jumping from planes and parachute towers erected in towns across the country. The Russians were also experimenting with the idea of parachuting entire units complete with vehicles and light tanks.

Russian paratroopers embarking a Tupolev TB-3 aircraft.

The Soviets were one of the first countries to take the concept of airborne infantry seriously; developing the tactics during the 1930s. In September 1935, a major Soviet exercise near Kiev demonstrated to Western military observers just how far Soviet airborne warfare had been developed. Their paratroopers would ascend in Tupolev TB-3 aircraft, which were capable of carrying up to 35 paratroops. Once over the drop zone, the parachutists would disembark by climbing up out of the top of the fuselage, dropping themselves down onto the plane's wing and then sliding off. To minimize drop-zone dispersion, the paratroopers were trained to wait until most of the men were on the wing before jumping. The Soviet paratroopers did not use static lines for these jumps.

At the Kiev demonstration, a U.S. observer reported that 1,800 paratroops jumped simultaneously with weapons and ammunition and formed a defensive strong point behind simulated enemy lines to be relieved by a Soviet tank column. A British observer at the exercise was indifferent; however, one country was universally impressed by the demonstration: Germany.

Russian airborne troops made relatively few combat jumps, since most were forced into ground battle as regular infantry soldiers when Germany invaded Russia in 1941. Most of the original Soviet

Russian paratroopers equipped to jump.

Russian paratroopers jumping from the wings of a Tupolev TB-3 aircraft. Notice how they are bunched on the wing to minimize drop-zone dispersion—and they are freefalling with no static lines.

paratroops were killed in the first months of the war, thus, no replacements were capable of making jumps until a year later. Russian paratroopers accomplished only two significant airborne operations during World War II. These were the Vyazma Airborne Operation during February-March 1942 and the Battle of Dnieper during September 1943. Both operations were inside the Soviet Union; and, owing to great losses, Dnieper became the last mass airborne operation accomplished by the Soviet Union during World War II.

As mentioned previously, a delegation from Germany attended the Kiev maneuvers in 1935 to observe with great interest. In little more than a year later, the German Luftwaffe quickly established a parachute school, and was allocated a number of Junker Ju 52 aircraft for training. These aircraft were slightly modified to accomplish paratroop transports.

The first *Fallschirmjäger* (paratroopers) training class commenced on 3 May 1936. Kurt Student was appointed the school's first commander, where he conceived and implemented a rapid deployment strike force by parachuting men, equipment, and weapons from aircraft. In

Russian paratroopers have emerged from inside the aircraft to line up closely together for the jump.

German Luftwaffe Ju 52s dropping paratroopers.

July 1938, by then a general officer, Student was named commanding general of the 7. Flieger-Division, Germany's first *Fallschirmjäger* division. Under his leadership, Germany demonstrated the effectiveness of airborne troops delivered into battle throughout World War II.

Other nations, including Argentina, Peru, Japan, France, and Poland also organized airborne units during the 1930's. France became the first nation to organize women in an airborne unit when they recruited and trained 200 nurses. During peace time, these nurses would be parachuted to support natural disasters. During conflict they would become a uniformed airborne medical unit.

Rare color photograph of German *Fallschirmjäger* jumping from a Luftwaffe Ju 52 over the countryside in Crete circa 1940.

# CHAPTER 4

# U.S. AIRBORNE DEVELOPMENT ACTIVITIES

On 24 September 1927, the first "mass" jump by U.S. military members was accomplished by five U.S. Marines and four U.S. Navy sailors from an altitude of 1,500 feet. The operation was conducted at Anacostia Flats in Washington, DC, now Anacostia Naval Air Station and home to the fleet of U.S. Marine helicopters that serve the President.

One year later, Brigadier General Billy Mitchell directed that six U.S. Army soldiers exit a Martin bomber aircraft by parachute with full-field equipment, land, and set-up a machine gun on the drop zone at Kelly Field, Texas (now part of Joint Base San Antonio). Mitchell was without question one of the most dominant and instrumental figures in military aviation during the post-World War I period.

As discussed previously, other countries (e.g., France, Russia, and Germany), had substantially developed "air-delivered forces" capabilities. It was not until June 1941 that General George C. Marshall directed the U.S. Army Infantry Board to commence training an all-volunteer Parachute Test Platoon. This came about as a result of the

General William "Billy" Mitchell, in 1932, in the cockpit of a Thomas Morse B-3A pursuit plane.

20 May 1941 Battle of Crete, where German paratroops were used in mass; making it the first largely airborne invasion in military history.

As a result of General Marshall's direction, a 50-man U.S. Army Parachute Test Platoon was established to develop tactics, techniques, and doctrine for airborne operations using a 28-foot T-4 static-line parachute. This platoon had "fantastic" success. The newly developed parachute was designed for low-altitude use by field-equipped soldiers. A smaller 22-foot back-up "reserve" parachute was used for emergency deployment in case of malfunction. Noteworthy is the fact that the U.S. Army was the first to equip troops with reserve parachutes, the only country to do so during World War II.

Operation MARKET GARDEN fought in the Netherlands in September 1944, remains the largest airborne battle in history.

Starting from that single test platoon, American airborne forces grew to a mighty force of five divisions and a number of smaller, independent paratrooper units. During the course of the war, five U.S. Army airborne divisions were created and activated. The five divisions were the 11th, 13th, 17th, 82nd, and 101st. Many of their World War II exploits became legendary. Operation TORCH in North Africa (Algeria, Morocco, Tunisia), was the first operation of the war using paratroopers. Other operations included Normandy, France;

General Eisenhower addressing troops in the 101st Airborne Division on the eve of Operation OVERLORD, the D-Day landings at Normandy, France on 6 June 1944.

World War II-era C-47 "Skytrains" dropping airborne troops.

Bastogne, Belgium; the raid at Cabanatuan, Philippines; and many other battlefields scattered across North Africa, Europe, and the Pacific.

With respect to parachuting, the U.S. Marine Corps didn't sit idle. In October 1940, the Commandant of the Marine Corp dispatched a letter to all USMC units to solicit volunteer paratroopers. To qualify, the volunteer had to be unmarried; an indication of the expected hazards of the duty. The letter further stated that personnel qualified as parachutists would receive an unspecified amount of extra pay. Parachute duty promised "plenty of action" and the chance to get in on the ground floor of a revolutionary type of warfare.

The first contingent of Marine trainees was sent to the Naval Air Station, Lakehurst, New Jersey for training later in October. Their initial training program included a 16-week course of instruction at the Parachute Material School. Upon graduation, each man was required to complete a requisite 10 jumps to qualify as a parachutist and parachute rigger. Several of these first graduates were retained at Lakehurst as instructors, while all others were sent to the Pacific to form the 1st Marine Parachute Battalion, which was activated on 1 April 1941 at Vella Lavella (an island in the Western Province of the Solomon Islands). They were assigned to the 1st Marine Amphibious Division.

Paramarine in training at the Naval Air Station, Lakehurst, New Jersey in 1940.

**PARACHUTING OUT OF THE SKIE** with COLUMBIA Compax Folding Bicycles come the "Leathernecks" of Uncle Sam's Marine Corps in spectacular tests of new tactics. In a matter of seconds, the "folded" bicycles are assembled and ready to speed away on a lightning-fast maneuver.

Vintage advertisement touting airborne capabilities of U.S. Marines.

Insignia of the 1st Marine Parachute Regiment.

A second group was trained in December 1940, forming the 2nd Marine Parachute Battalion. A third contingent trained at Camp Kearney near San Diego in early 1941; eventually forming the 3rd Marine Parachute Battalion. These three parachute battalions, with approximately 3,000 men, collectively formed the 1st Marine Parachute Regiment of the I Marine Amphibious Corps (called I MAC). Four parachute operations were planned during World War II, but never undertaken.

During the post-war period, the Marine Corps quickly disbanded its parachute battalions; largely because of a lack of money to sustain the mission, and because they lacked the essential transport aircraft. The U.S. Army, in spite of post-war depletion of money and men, retained the capability and built a training and support infrastructure that would benefit the UDT and SEAL Teams in the future.

# CHAPTER 5

# WWII PARACHUTING OSS STYLE

## Office of Strategic Services - JEDBURGs

In his book *The Shadow War Against Hitler: The Covert Operations of America's Wartime Secret Intelligence Service*, Jeremiah Riemer concludes that the Office of Strategic Services (OSS) contributed materially to the Allied cause by, among other things, targeting and exploiting weak points in the German economy, identifying bombing targets, disrupting civilian and military morale, and spreading misinformation that helped pin down Wehrmacht and SS units that might otherwise have gone into battle against the Allies. Jeremiah Riemer's words provided a vivid description of the actions and activities of the JEDBURGs, whom most prominently used parachuting as a means of clandestine infiltration. JEDBURG operations were planned and conducted by the OSS Secret Intelligence Branch in London in coordination with the British Special Operations Executive.

The name JEDBURGH was derived from a small town in Scotland. JEDBURGH was a series of tightly planned clandestine and covert special operations carried out by the Allies during World War II. JEDBURGH operations, actions, and activities were aimed to coordinate the engagements of the Resistance with the general plans of the Supreme Headquarters Allied Expeditionary Forces. The objective was to provide weapons and training to the Resistance in France, Belgium, and the Netherlands, and to prevent German capabilities to reinforce the Normandy coast at the time of D-Day. Men and women of the British Special Operations Executive, American OSS, Free French Bureau Central de Renseignements et d'Action, as well as soldiers of the various armies of the countries concerned, were infiltrated by air or waterborne methods. Generally, teams of three were parachuted in uniform behind the German lines to lead actions of sabotage and guerrilla activities against the Germans, and to coordinate Resistance actions. It was also not unusual for some teams to be parachuted in civilian clothes for covert operations. About 100

JEDBURGH teams were dropped into France, Belgium, and Netherlands between June and December 1944.

Many readers won't know that there is a difference between "covert" and "clandestine" activities with regard to the U.S. military. It is often said that clandestine operations are intended to hide the deed and not the doer, while covert operations are intended to hide the doer and not the deed.

The formal definitions may be found in the U.S. Department of Defense Dictionary of Military and Associated Terms, which describes a covert activity as: "An operation that is so planned and executed as to conceal the identity of or permit plausible denial by the sponsor." Most covert activities are intended to create a political effect, which can have implications in military intelligence; affecting either the internal population of a country or individuals outside of it. The same DoD dictionary defines a clandestine operation as: "An operation sponsored or conducted by governmental departments or agencies in such a way as to assure secrecy or concealment. A clandestine operation differs from a covert operation in that emphasis is placed on concealment of the operation rather than on concealment of the identity of the sponsor." Within special operations (i.e., Navy SEALs or Army Special Forces), an activity may be both covert and clandestine and may focus equally on operational considerations and intelligence-related activities.

Parachute operations were employed extensively by OSS Operational Groups, which also conducted numerous clandestine operations in the Middle East Theater of Operations, most notably into the Austrian area of the Balkans. By the summer of 1944, the Allies had Italy completely contained, and were continuing a long and bloody advance toward Germany. Allied and OSS operations were being coordinated out of Bari, Italy, where the focus of sabotage and information gathering had shifted further north to the Third Reich itself.

Within the OSS, there were many unsung heroes, however, by virtue of training and operations there was, objectively, one individual of the U. S. Navy who accomplished the full range of clandestine and covert maritime special operations, actions, and activities, now considered core to the SEAL Teams. His foremost parachute operation was the DUPONT mission, and he was Navy Lieutenant Jack Taylor, USNR.

## America's First Sea-Air-Land Commando

When the U.S. entered World War II, Jack Taylor was a 33-year old orthodontist practicing in California. When the war broke out, he joined the Navy as a line officer and initially served on a sub-chaser. Based on his vast pre-war experience as an open-ocean sailor, he was sequestered by the OSS to serve in their newly formed Maritime Section as an instructor in boat handling, navigation, and seamanship. The Maritime Section eventually obtained branch status as the OSS Maritime Unit (OSS MU), and Jack Taylor went on to become the first OSS MU officer to train with the Lambertsen Amphibious Respiratory Unit (LARU), a pure oxygen-rebreather and the nation's first practical underwater breathing apparatus. Noteworthy is the fact that he set an early record by being the first to swim one mile underwater with the LARU. Lieutenant Taylor was subsequently assigned to the

OSS and Navy Lieutenant Jack Taylor became the first officer deployed by the OSS Maritime Unit as head of MU operations in the Middle East Theater of Operations. In this photograph, he is seen with one of his indigenous Greek crews.

"L-Unit," the first OSS MU swimmer group trained and selected for deployment to the European Theater of Operations.

Before deployment to England, however, his vast experience in small boat operations found another calling, and he was transferred to the Cairo, Egypt to become the first OSS MU representative in the Middle East. Over a 15-month period, his achievements were considerable in the landing of agents and the delivery of ammunition and supplies to advance operations bases in the Nazi-occupied Greek Islands and mainland, and into Yugoslavia and Albania; including near capture on one occasion.

In the Autumn of 1944, it was recognized that there were no known partisan groups or resistance movements in Austria with whom to ally. Thus, the Vienna area was chosen as a top first priority for infiltration of an OSS team. Lieutenant Taylor was selected to lead

Jack Taylor is seen with the star and crescent moon flag that was flown by many Islamic countries in the Mediterranean during WWII. He led numerous clandestine ferrying operations into German-occupied territory using Greek crews piloting Greek boats called *caiques*.

Jack Taylor seen in his prison uniform some time after his liberation from the death camp at Mauthausen.

three volunteer Austrian corporal POWs on the first American operation into Austria; coined the DUPONT Mission.

On 13 October 1944, his four-man team was infiltrated by parachute using  a British Liberator bomber aircraft manned by a Polish crew. To minimize their exposure to searchlights and anti-aircraft batteries, the jump was planned to be conducted during the dark of the moon from an altitude of 400 feet; without a ground reception committee or ground lights, and with absolutely no circling. Compared to normal partisan drops, this plan was entirely abnormal, due to the extremely hazardous nature of the operation.

The jump was accomplished, but not without difficulties. Foremost was that the supply bundle containing the mission's radio communications landed in a lake and could not be recovered. The clandestine information-gathering mission continued under this and other adverse conditions.

After evading the enemy for over six weeks, the entire team was captured and interned in a Vienna prison. Lieutenant Taylor was later sent to the Mauthausen extermination camp (instead of a concentration or prisoner of war camp), where he was severely tortured and brutalized at arguably the most notorious of all the Nazi death camps. He was scheduled to be executed on 28 April 1945, but three days before a friendly Czech

LCDR Jack Taylor testifying at the Mauthausen-Gusen Camp Trials. Of all his awards and decorations, he chose to wear only his jump wings.

working in the political department burned his file. Several days later, Mauthausen was liberated by the Americans, and Lieutenant Taylor was set free.

Jack Taylor would, however, perform one final mission, and perhaps his most important. He was recalled to active duty in March 1946, promoted to Lieutenant Commander, and sent back to Germany to serve as a primary witness for the prosecution at the Mauthausen-Gusen Camp Trials (a subset of the Nuremberg Trials), which were held at the Dachau Concentration Camp. Jack Taylor testified wearing his Navy Service Dress Blue uniform with silver jump wings over his left breast pocket.

As a member of the U.S. Navy, Lieutenant Commander Jack Taylor unquestionably stands out in the history of maritime special operations as our nation's first sea, air, and land commando. While he didn't have the benefit of today's formal training, parachuting or otherwise, his operational exploits and personal daring continue serve as a role model for present day SEALs to emulate. Sadly, in May 1959, Jack Taylor was killed in a light plane, which stalled and crashed on approach to the airport near El Centro, California. A friend riding as a passenger with him was also killed in the crash.

# CHAPTER 6

# UDT PARACHUTING INNOVATIONS

Today, basic and advanced parachuting in the SEAL, SEAL Delivery Vehicle (SDV), and Special Boat Teams (SBTs) is accepted as a routine part of doing business. While the parachuting lineage of today's Naval Special Warfare (NSW) forces can be traced to the early 1950s, advances after World War II were, for the most part, accomplished by the U.S. Army. The Marines did away with parachuting after the war, as discussed in a previous chapter. Advances in freefall parachuting, however, came largely from sport parachuting clubs, and this is how it began for the SEAL Teams.

Naval Special Warfare's mastery of the air, which today is unmatched by any other military units, had its beginnings in a time of sparse funding, little logistical support, and with little to no recognition or support by the "Big Navy." Innovation and determination was what made things happen.

A UDT frogman exits a Grumman HU-16 C/D Albatross in the 1950s wearing swim fins.

Photo of the same Grumman HU-16 C/D Albatross showing the UDT operator's parachute being deployed.

UDT operator making a static-line parachute jump. Note the tight body position as he exits the aircraft.

In the years after World War II, if it wasn't a ship, submarine, or aircraft, our Navy didn't know what to do with it. Of the various specialized units established during World War II to scout coastlines and clear the way for amphibious assaults, only the Underwater Demolition Teams (UDT) survived doctrinally, and just barely. (As will be seen, the UDTs were the precursors to today's U.S. Navy SEAL and SEAL Delivery Vehicle Teams.)

From the outset, UDTs never fit well within the Navy, because they were very small units that meant really nothing in the Navy's big picture after the war in the Pacific. They were, for the most part, simply small units with a vital amphibious warfare mission that few outside the UDT community itself really understood or appreciated. The post-war UDTs were always fighting for survival, and had very small budgets with which to train and operate. Without senior officers, the UDTs had nobody in the Navy hierarchy looking out for their needs or best interests. UDT budgets were almost routinely cut, and manning billets were likewise reduced; often to bare minimums to maintain basic operational capabilities. The senior leadership at every command level consistently tried to take bits and pieces out of the little UDTs, because they were considered easy pickings. During this period, the Navy's leadership considered it adverse to pick on submarines, aviation, or ships, thus, when times were tough, the

UDTs and other small units were where they went to make budget cuts to fund other "more important" Navy activities.

This didn't deter the UDT men at all. In fact, it undoubtedly strengthened their resolve. The UDT officers and men had little or nothing, but loved the challenges in spite of the hardships. On the favorable side, no one bothered the UDTs in their day-to-day business. The men would beg, borrow, and surely steal if they needed to, and would take anything they could get – more often than not, living out of the Navy's salvage yards. In that kind of environment, the UDT men were always looking for ways to be useful and always to survive. That mentality created a fertile ground for innovation.

In the Spring of 1950, five years after the close of World War II, and during the early period of the Korean Police Action, the Office of the Chief of Naval Operations (CNO) requested that the Commanders of Underwater Demolition Units ONE and TWO (COMUDUONE and COMUDUTWO) submit a list of qualified UDT officers recommended for specialized training at Fort Benning, Georgia. This training would require, among other things, qualification as parachutists. (Note: The commanders of the Underwater Demolition Units were the senior UDT officer in command of UDT-1 and UDT-3 on the West Coast and UDT-2 and UDT-4 on the East Coast.)

In January 1951, Lieutenant Bruce Dunning from UDT-2 at the Naval Amphibious Base (NAB) Little Creek, Norfolk, Virginia was the first UDT operator selected to attend this specialized, tri-service training. After graduation the following February, and while in route to Washington, DC, Lieutenant Dunning briefed COMUDUTWO on the value of having Basic Airborne Training incorporated into the UDT program; both as a delivery means and to upgrade the quality of UDT training. Lieutenant Bill Thede from UDT-1 at NAB, Coronado, California attended the next class, and he was followed by Lieutenant Junior Grade Allen Jones, Jr. from UDT-4.

It is not clear whether others from UDT attended this specialized training during the Korean War, but the returning men continued to recommend that the UDT should add basic airborne training to the UDT program. In a number of cases, as this training progressed, it led to assignment with the Central Intelligence Agency, the follow-on organization to the OSS after it was disbanded at the end of World War II. Qualification as a parachutist was a prerequisite for such assignments.

During a periodic review of the UDT doctrinal mission, Commander Leo Huddleston comprehended that parachuting was envisioned as mission-essential.

In 1954, the commanding officer of UDT-21, Lieutenant Leo Huddleston (a World War II veteran of UDT-13 in the Pacific), was tasked to review the UDT mission statement, which was required to be accomplished periodically. It surprised him to find it stated that the UDTs should have the capability of getting to an objective area by parachute. The pioneers in the early naval commando units undoubtedly saw the value of parachuting in their interactions with European commandos and OSS operators, and left an open door for what is now a core and mission-essential readiness capability in SEAL training. (Note: UDT-21 was previously known as UDT-2. The numbering system for all UDTs was changed after Korea. UDT-1 and UDT-3 became UDT-11 and UDT-12. UDT-4 became UDT-22.)

With this discovery, Lieutenant Huddleston wasted no time in recommending that a select number of UDT men acquire parachute training: "To see if it was in fact a viable option." It took a year of persistent struggle with the U.S. Army to finally get quotas to their Basic Airborne School at Fort Benning, Georgia. In the fall of 1955, Commander Dave Saunders, COMUDUTWO (Commanding Officer of World War II UDT-26 in the Pacific), and Lieutenant Larry Fay from UDT-22 also headed to Ft. Benning. As those two men commenced training, Lieutenant Huddleston and Lieutenant Junior Grade Ralph Leonard, both of UDT-21, were given spots in the very next class.

Unfortunately, Commander Saunders was unable to complete the course and graduate due to a near fatal injury sustained on the Army's 250-foot training tower. As he was being hoisted up, the locking mechanism that secured the apex of the parachute assembly prematurely released at about 100 feet, driving him to the ground and severely injuring one of his ankles. He was subsequently retired on full disability. This was the first tower malfunction in the history of the U.S. Army's Airborne

The Army's 250-foot high Training Tower. Trainees are lifted to the top and released to practice the PLF or parachute landing fall; a technique to land safely without undue injury.

training program, which is phenomenal when considering that nearly a quarter of a million trainees had passed through the "Cradle of American Airborne" before him. As a result, those that followed were hooked up to a safety line that attached to the solid outer ring housing each of the tower's canopies.

After returning from Fort Benning, Commander Saunders was convinced that all UDT frogmen should take to the air, and immediately began campaigning for more quotas. Airborne school is, and always has been, a big luxury in the Army, with hundreds of soldiers trying to get in. To make it even tougher on the UDT men at the time, the Navy brass at the Pentagon, were pondering: "Why do demolition divers need to go to Army jump school?" Quotas were very hard to obtain, but the UDTs were very adept in scrounging and just didn't quit. It took a while to get more quotas, but they ultimately succeeded.

Following this initial assessment, quotas were granted for 15 frogmen in the spring of 1956. Their purpose was to complete the training and return to Little Creek to develop tactical water-entry techniques. When the call went out to UDT-21 and UDT-22 for volunteers, virtually everyone signed up—including me. Lieutenant Junior Grade Leonard was placed in charge of pairing this group down to three officers and 12 enlisted men. After several weeks, the selections were made and I was selected as the detachment officer in charge. The extended story is told in the next chapter.

# CHAPTER 7

# THE DIRTY DOZEN PLUS THREE

In 1956, the first large group of UDT frogmen were screened to attend the U.S. Army Basic Airborne Course "Jump School" at Fort Benning, Georgia. Twelve enlisted men and three officer slots were allocated ergo, the Dirty Dozen plus Three.

The period of pre-screening, coined by fellow teammate Frank Moncrief, was "Gladiator Training." It involved untold numbers of pull-ups, practicing the "Parachute Shuffle" and worse yet, wearing starched Army greens, polishing brass, shaving one's head and learning how to march. After several weeks, the selection was made and I was designated as officer-in-in charge of the detachment. Although there was much complaining during this pre-screening phase, it paid off, making the actual training a piece of cake.

In those days, the UDTs wore "boon dockers," which were high-topped leather shoes that we wore for everything—including running in the surf—and WWII-vintage Seabee greens

UDT-21 at Basic Airborne Course, Class 12, Fort Benning, Georgia on 19 June 1956. Standing (l-r) Olson, Prahm, DiMartino, Bond, McAllister, Boitnot, Moncrief, Grimes, Connelly. Kneeling: Salerno, Robbins, McGee, Ballard, Sulinski, Steimle.

with soft billed caps. In most cases, these uniforms had been turned in by departing frogmen and reissued to newly arrived trainees. Last names were stenciled over one of the pockets and new arrivals usually had several iterations of names that had been blackened out before re-issue. The bottom line was that this ensemble, referred to as a uniform, was motley looking at best.

In preparation for jump school, however, and to the dismay of others in the unit, we acquired several sets of Army-style green uniforms purchased at nearby Fort Story.

Brown Corcoran® jump boots from the early 1950s

## NAVY UDT MEMBERS OF ARMY AIRBORNE CLASS 12

### THE "DIRTY DOZEN PLUS THREE"

**Graduated June 1956**

LTjg Norman Olson, Detachment Officer-in-Charge
LTjg Jack Connelly
Ensign Tony Steimle
BM1 Joe DiMartino
BM1 Fred "Robby" Robbins
QM1 Charles "Moose" Boitnott
GM1 Ben Sulinski*
MN1 Jim McGee
CD1 Paul Grimes*
GM2 Tom McAllister
MM2 "Charlie" Bond
EM2 Frank Moncrief
BM3 Bob Salernoz
SW3 Bob Ballard
IC3 Dick Prahm
*Class honor men among 250 class members

Additionally, we had to pay for Corcoran® jump boots, without which we could not attend the course. In those days, the boots only came in brown, the color of the Army Airborne. Thus prior to departure, we had to dye them black, because only pilots were authorized to wear brown footwear in the Navy. All of the men used their own funds for these airborne necessities and uniform upgrades.

Basic Airborne Training had not changed much over the years, especially the jump platform and parachute. The aircraft was the C-119 "Flying Boxcar," and the parachute assembly was a T-10 with an unmodified 35- foot canopy. The first two weeks included ground training, while the third week consisted of five parachute jumps.

Airborne Class 12 graduated in June 1956. The parade review was marked with the UDT officers wearing khakis and framed caps and the enlisted men wearing a whites blouse,

Parachute trainees boarding a C-119.

Airborne trainees lined up in a "stick," to jump from the airplane. Note their parachute static lines clipped to the cable above their heads. When they jumped, the gravity of their fall would pull the static line and open their parachute.

neckerchief, and a "Dixie Cup" for headgear. Trousers were bloused above the jump boots.

It wasn't clear why our detachment was dispersed throughout the 250-man formation, but rumor had it that the Army didn't want our small group to stand out from the rest, particularly since the two class honor men were our UDT men: CM1 Ben Sulinsky and CD1 Paul Grimes. In truth, the Army probably feared that the UDT's marching skills would cause great hilarity and embarrassment, and that it would be far better if the enlisted men, in their dress whites, were spread out amongst the masses. A good decision!

Airborne Class 12 Honor Graduates Paul Grimes and Benny Sulinski.

Several sticks of parachutists are seen exiting C-119 "Flying Boxcars" flying in formation.

The enlisted members of the graduating class (l-r): Moncrief, Prahm, McAllister, Bond, Sulinksi, Boitnot, Grimes, Robbins, DiMartino, McGee, Salerno, and Ballar. Note that the bellbottom trousers are bloused Army style.

The officers of the graduating class (l-r): Detachment Officer-in-Charge LTjg Norman Olson, LTjg Jack Connelly, and Ensign Tony Steimle.

Following graduation, our detachment remained for an additional week of jumpmaster training, which included three more jumps. During this time, exits were made from the 34-foot tower wearing a dry suit with facemask and fins, either worn or secured at the beltline. Additionally, exits were made with the Draeger Closed Circuit SCUBA worn under the harness.

This preliminary assessment was done in anticipation of making water jumps once the detachment returned to Little Creek, Virginia. We needed to know what kind of impact the diving equipment would have on the parachute equipment. Unfortunately, however, budget cuts

LT Olson wearing the Army's green fatigue uniform adopted by the UDT Teams following graduation from Army Airborne Training.

Paul Grimes wearing a dry suit with swim fins attached to the leg straps of the parachute harness.

Paul Grimes exiting the 34-foot training tower with dry suit, fins, and face mask.

prevented us from making water jumps for the next four years. Being experts at working around difficulties and taking the initiative, we found ways to keep making progress without actually conducting jumps.

During this same period, I was tasked to develop techniques and evaluate procedures for water entry by parachute. Without benefit of aircraft or parachutes, this initial evaluation was limited to pool testing wearing salvaged parachute harnesses, and using something called the "Dilbert Dunker," a training device for naval aviators located at the Norfolk Naval Air Station several miles from our base at Little Creek. The name was derived from a World War II cartoon character name Dilbert the Pilot. Dilbert was a slang term in the Navy used to refer to a sailor who was foul-up or a screwball. This "Underwater Cockpit Escape Device" was used to train pilots to safely get out of aircraft that had been ditched in the water. The trainer would slide down a 45 degree rail at 25 mph, hit the water, and sink to the bottom of the deep pool. This device provided us the opportunity for innovation.

Although not like parachuting into the ocean, we felt that the Dilbert Dunker would be helpful in teaching us how to coordinate getting out of the parachute harness and donning the breathing apparatus. We figured we would be below the water for a while and wanted to have the feeling of being submerged and having to expedite becoming operational. Although this was far from ideal, the test did conclude that wearing a closed-circuit SCUBA and ancillary equipment under the existing parachute assembly was not the way to go, and that we needed some form of general purpose container.

The Dilbert Dunker hit the water at 25 miles per hour.

We discovered early on that the whole thing was pretty complicated. The Draeger diving apparatus had breathing bags, hoses and many connections, and the parachute itself had several straps and snaps. When you jump into the water you have to figure out how to get the parachute off, fins and facemask on, and diving apparatus activated. We also put considerable stress on the parachute assembly with a 180 pound UDT operator, inflatable boat, fins, SCUBA equipment, weapons, ammunition, radio, and rations. Some of the operators could easily top out at 400 pounds.

Without benefit of making actual water jumps, we surmised we would have to jump with a deployment bag that would be released from the harness on a tether, and that it would hit the water or ground first; leaving the jumper to land unconstrained. Unfortunately, live tests would not occur for four more years. During these subsequent years, other priorities and deployments took center stage, and they involved many of the original "Dirty Dozen."

In my case, I was first deployed for seven months to the Antarctic to support Operation DEEP FREEZE II; followed by a six-month deployment with the Amphibious Ready Group in the Mediterranean; culminating with three months supporting a joint UDT-Explosive Ordnance Disposal (EOD) diving operation near Tybee Island (near Savanna, Georgia). This deployment involved searching for a nuclear weapon that had been jettisoned following a mid-air collision between an Air Force B-47 Bomber and an F-86 Fighter jet on 5 February 1958. The weapon has never been recovered.

When I returned to UDT-21 in the early spring of 1958, I was assigned as the Team's operation's officer. Shortly thereafter, we arranged for 18 quotas to the Basic Airborne Course at Fort Benning, Georgia. In preparation for the course, a new group of volunteers commenced "Gladiator" pre-screening; this time under my watchful eye. The detachment was headed by Lieutenant Junior Grade Fred Cook, and they did extremely well in the eyes of the Army instructors.

During Operational DEEP FREEZE II, Olson recorded the first SCUBA dive in the Antarctic at Cape Hallett on New Year's Eve 1956. (Photo: *National Geographic*)

Subsequently, I was advanced to serve as the command's executive officer, and in late 1958, I visited the 7th Special Forces Group at Fort Bragg, North Carolina seeking an opportunity for 15 of our frogmen to attend their one week Airborne Orientation Course. This request was granted. Rigging and aerial delivery techniques unique to small unit units were demonstrated, followed by 11 jumps from a variety of fixed wing and rotary wing aircraft that included: H–19, H–21, L-20, SA-16 and C-123.

In return, the Green Berets wanted us to provide them closed-circuit SCUBA training at Little Creek, which was approved. This exchange was the first between Special Forces and the East Coast UDTs, and ultimately led to a very close working relationship once SEAL Team TWO was established in 1962.

Fortunately, this short interface with the 77th Special Forces Group allowed us to meet the XVIII Airborne Corps Strategic Army Corps Parachute Team, later to become the Army Parachute Team–"Golden Knights. They were conducting freefall parachute training adjacent to us at the same drop-zone. Subsequent personal contact allowed the

UDT men made two jumps from an L-20 (top), one from an SA-16 (middle) and one from a C-123 (bottom).

UDT men made five jumps from a H-19 helicopter and two from an H-21 helicopter

UDTs to exploit advances in freefall parachuting, which are discussed in Chapter 9.

Around the same time, Underwater Demolition Unit TWO validated their mission statement, followed by the submission of the command's allowance list for Army T-10 main and reserve parachute assemblies and related support equipment to the Department of the Navy. The lengthy approval process was caused by a combination of three factors: authorizing the funding source; processing this unique and non-traditional request; and coordinating it with another branch of service.

This U.S. Army Parachute Rigger patch was worn by qualified UDT Riggers on the left breast pocket of their fatigue uniforms.

Finally, the parachute allowances were approved, additional quotas to the Basic Airborne Course, Fort Benning, Georgia were obtained, and a quonset hut in the UDT headquarters compound was outfitted with packing tables and assorted support equipment. Additionally, a number of qualified parachute personnel were selected to attend the U.S. Army Parachute Rigger School, Fort Lee, Virginia to understand fabrics, hardware, webbing, regulations, sewing, packing, and other aspects related to the building, packing, repair, and maintenance of parachutes.

The C-1A Trader was a U.S. Navy carrier onboard delivery (COD) aircraft. This airplane was capable of delivering eight jumpers from its side door.

In 1960, six qualified UDT jumpers were tasked to conduct 60 water jumps each to test and develop tactics and techniques for airborne delivery of parachutists in support of maritime operations. Lieutenant Junior Grade "Solly" Mimms was designated officer in charge, and his men included: BM1 "Robby" Robins, TM1 "Pat" Patterson, MR1 Ken Lange, DM1 "Lenny" Waugh, and SM2 Bill Bruhmuller.

To conduct these tests, Oceana Naval Air Station was tasked to provide C-1A aircraft,

Quonset huts like this one were readily available throughout the Little Creek Naval Amphibious Base.

rigger support, and a parachute loft with a drying tower. Army Riggers from the XVIII Airborne Corps provided training in T-10 parachute packing to the station's Navy riggers.

The immediate challenge was to design and fabricate watertight GP (general purpose) bags out of old ponchos, parachute webbing, and flotation bladders. Salvage depots were an excellent source of materials and hardware. With limited funds and virtually no logistics support, our men embarked on this pioneering effort through determination and innovation at the grass roots level. Once prototypes were fabricated, individual jumpers tested the various concepts with load variations, e.g., SCUBA, weapons, ammunition, explosives, etc.

Once that first step was proven, the next challenge was how to jump with a seven-man Inflatable Boat Small (IBS) weighing 365 pounds. It couldn't be jumped inflated, so it had to be rolled up and secured to the jumper. The first jumps were made with the boat strapped to the jumper's chest. He had to be pushed out of the plane's door, enter the water with the boat, ditch the parachute, and then inflate the boat. This process was dangerous and life threatening, and was abandoned in short order.

A SEAL Team operator making a jump with a modified T-10 parachute using a General Purpose equipment bag.

Subsequently, the jumper would exit the plane in the same configuration with the boat secured to his chest. As soon as the canopy inflated, he would release the boat on a tether secured to his harness. When the boat hit the water, he would then release the tether, ditch the parachute, swim to the boat, and manually inflate it. Later on, the men were able to rig the boat so that it would automatically inflate when it hit the water.

Once this technique was perfected, the entire boat crew would exit the plane and rendezvous at the boat in the water. The individual jumpers would carry everything to man the boat and accomplish the mission, e.g., paddles, weapons, ammunition, explosives, and oftentimes the outboard motor. These pioneering efforts during the late 50s and early 60s contributed significantly to the growth of today's Naval Special Warfare "Air" capability.

Reflecting back to this era, parachuting was an alien concept to many of the older frogmen, and many simply dismissed it as a passing fancy. It was, however, of great interest to the younger frogmen, who volunteered in mass when the opportunity first presented itself to attend jump school. Many of the older UDT men chose not to attend. Also, many that did had mixed emotions about jumping. Some loved it and some disliked it, but the majority accepted it as a necessary part of being a Navy frogman. Extra hazardous-duty pay came with parachuting, and liking parachuting or not, they did like the extra money in their paychecks.

Following this embryonic stage of development, jumping slowly became a part of UDT's culture. Naval Special Warfare's leadership for many years, however, had no clear vision as to how to employ parachuting effectively in the maritime environment. In large part, it was because parachuting was not clearly defined as a UDT mission.

This general malaise toward parachuting came slowly to rest with the establishment of Navy SEAL Teams. Their mission—Sea, Air, Land—clearly defines the environments in which they operate and in the air, ergo, parachuting, became one in which they excel.

Following the aforementioned tests, I was transferred to reserve status and subsequently to the Atlantic Fleet's Amphibious Force Flagship as Chief Engineer. Transfers like this were common for officers, because

Members of SEAL Team TWO combat ready and posting behind their reserve parachutes, circa 1962. Notice the man standing second from the left is fully rigged and in a ready to jump configuration.

UDT was not considered a career enhancing duty assignment. I was deployed to the Caribbean and the Mediterranean, and participated in the Cuban Blockade during the Missile Crisis. I was promoted to Lieutenant Commander; and, fortunately for my next assignment, I was detailed as the Commanding Officer of UDT-11 on the West Coast. There I got back into parachuting, forming and leading what today is known as the U.S. Navy Parachute Team —Leap Frogs, and this is discussed in Chapter 10.

UDT operators preparing to board a Navy C-1A Trader to make a water jump wearing open circuit SCUBA gear.

# CHAPTER 8

# PARACHUTING: UDTS PACIFIC

In the previous chapter, the UDT's parachuting origins focused on the men on the East Coast, however, the West Coast UDT men were certainly not idle or passive. The story of the West Coast UDTs is also a story of substantial personal initiative and working around obstacles.

The East Coast UDTs had somewhat of a luxury of being able to go to Fort Benning for basic airborne training, and later the luck of having Army Special Forces down in Fort Bragg, North Carolina with whom the UDTs would quickly affiliate. It was much, much harder to find a way to parachute for the Coronado-based UDTs. Their need to consistently scrounge for all kinds of equipment led to the development of parachuting on the West Coast, not in their homeport of Coronado, but across the Pacific in Japan.

The East and West Coast UDTs were worlds apart and rarely, if ever, communicated. In fact, there was always an undercurrent of competition among the Teams, which is many respects was a healthy path toward innovation. Word got around that the East Coast UDTs were jumping out of planes, and the West Coast men wanted to do it too. Using the Army Airborne School at Fort Benning was out of the question, so the men took the initiative and wangled some quotas at the U.S. Army's Test Station in Yuma, Arizona. Later, through informal "back channel" connections with Army Special Forces, they were able to elbow their way into the door at an Army Air base on Okinawa, Japan.

It was commonplace for UDTs deployed in the Western Pacific to request quotas for special training from the Army 1st Special Forces Group stationed in Japan. In early 1962, Lieutenant Junior Grade George Raines, the deployed Officer in Charge of UDT-11's Second Platoon, Detachment Mike, received the news that his platoon of two officers and 13 enlisted men would be the first on the West Coast to receive parachute training. In exchange, they would provide their 1st Army Special Forces Group (SFG) counterparts SCUBA training.

A new airborne trainee in Japan is tapped as a signal to jump by the Army instructor.

Airborne trainees jumping from the 34-foot tower on Okinawa.

Airborne trainees learning proper parachuting techniques.

Airborne trainees practicing in in the swing-landing trainer.

Like the men from the East Coast UDTs, they had to buy their own uniforms, equipment, and expensive boots. The Navy paid for nothing. Still, the platoon deployed from Yokosuka, Japan to Okinawa with a lot of enthusiasm and anticipation. They arrived in typical UDT fashion with no money, no billeting, and a long list of requirements. The platoon's Chief Petty Officer was Chief Photographer's Mate (PHC) Gene "Gag" Gagliardi. As luck would have it, Chief Gagliardi had for many years before been involved with training the 1st Special Forces Group in SCUBA at Camp McGill, Japan and was already jump qualified. As a result, he used his network of contacts to obtain billeting at Camp Sukeran. A week or so prior to training, the platoon received a list of required exercises from the Army, thereby allowing them to "fine tune" their physical fitness program following the Army school's requirements.

The day before the course was to start, Lieutenant Junior Grade Raines was informed that SEVENTH Fleet staff had approved his request to train the platoon in parachuting, however, that the approval was for only two officers and five enlisted men. This caused significant consternation on both sides. The Army's 1st Special Forces Group was in a time crunch and could not afford to train only seven personnel, and the UDT platoon was faced with a morale problem, because the men had paid for their personal equipment, trained hard, and were fired up and ready to go. With no time to go through channels, the problem, in typical UDT fashion, was solved with the stroke of a pen, by inserting the number "one" in front of the five, thus, transforming the quota back to the 15 requested.

Because the platoon was so highly motivated and in such good physical shape, the course was compressed from five weeks to two, and the five qualifying jumps, all accomplished from a helicopter, were completed in just one day. EM3 Duane McDonald was injured during training and could not complete the course, thus, two officers and 12 enlisted men graduated on 31 March 1961. It was quite a milestone for the UDT men. As luck would have it, however, their training was considered unique and of interest

## UDT-11, SECOND PLATOON

### DETACHMENT MIKE

**Trained with 1st Special Forces Group, Okinawa
Graduated August 31, 1961**

LTjg George Raines, Detachment Officer-in-Charge
LTjg Ted Hammond
PHC Gene Gagliardi
SF1 Bob Fisher
SF1 Billy Steward
QM2 Clarence Betz
MN2 Gordon Brown
GM2 Frank Goerlich
GM2 Charlie Nelson
GM2 Joe Sehion
EN2 Billy Davis
SK2 Don "Herky" Hertenstein
RM2 Harry Monahan
MR3 Nick Dana
SN Curtis Hall
SN Bill Okesson
* EM3 Duane McDonald did not graduate

n the military. As a consequence, the new graduates were featured on the front page of the next issue of the *Stars and Stripes* magazine, which was read by virtually everyone connected with the U.S. Armed Forces in the Western Pacific, and, in fact, the world.

When the SEVENTH Fleet staff officers learned the details of the UDT's parachute training, Lieutenant Junior Grade Raines was immediately ordered to report to the flagship to explain how so many personnel had undergone jump training without authorization. There is no known record of Lieutenant Junior Grade Raines' response to the staff, but rarely is a Navy junior grade lieutenant called on the carpet before senior officers not directly in his chain of command to explain his activities. Such matters are generally the domain of the

The men of Detachment Mike that trained with the 1st Special Forces Group in Okinawa, August 1961.

UDT operators Jim Batton and "Doc" Baker display what it's like to be fully rigged for a land warfare static line combat jump.

deployed senior officer in command, in this case the Amphibious Force Commander, or, if more appropriate, the individual's commanding officer. While Lieutenant Junior Grade Raines' encounter with three Navy captains didn't result in an official reprimand, it can be said that his unofficial admonition surely ranked among the highest for a junior UDT officer in the 1960s—and perhaps ever. Raines and his men had falsified records and deserved the chewing out, but, in the end, UDT-11 got several men parachute-qualified and, from that perspective, they felt it was worth it. And, despite the turmoil surrounding that first training class, a precedent was set. From then on, all UDT platoons in the Western Pacific had the opportunity to qualify as basic parachutists at the 1st Special Forces Group School at Camp Sukeran, Okinawa.

After returning to the U.S. after the deployment, Chief "Gag" Gagliardi continued on to qualify as a jumpmaster and instructor at the U.S. Army's Test Station in Yuma, Arizona and as a Parachute Rigger at Fort Lee, Virginia. Subsequently, he, along with DC1 Ed Reynolds, SM2 Joe Messenger, and SK2 "Herky" Hertenstein qualified in High Altitude, Low Opening (HALO) techniques, also at Yuma. It was this cadre that established the foundation for all follow-on parachuting on the West Coast.

While the infrastructure for parachuting had been established, access to jump training for West Coast UDT personnel was sporadic and unpredictable. However, as Commanding Officer UDT-11, I was able to obtain quotas in February 1965 for 24 operators from UDT-11 and UDT-12 to attend Basic Airborne Class 25 at Fort

The UDT men of Basic Airborne Class 25 at Fort Benning received the first group award ever presented for Outstanding Team Leadership.

Benning, Georgia. I also insured that the men would run a West Coast version of "Gladiator" training that had worked so well on the East Coast. Lieutenat Jim Batton was selected as the detachment officer-in-charge. The superb performance of this detachment led to presentation of the first and only group award ever given by the Airborne Department for Outstanding Team Leadership.

With the growing requirement for all UDT personnel to be parachute qualified, additional quotas for Basic Airborne Training became a necessary. At the same time, the Vietnam War was escalating and the need for Navy SEALs was growing as well. As a result, a select group of UDT-11/12 personnel with parachute qualifications were transferred to fill the needs in SEAL Team ONE. Members of UDT-11 and UDT-12 had to be qualified parachutists in order to be considered for selection as a SEAL. This compounded the need for additional airborne quotas exponentially. Responding to these urgent and concurrent demands, I worked to acquire these additional quotas at Fort Benning until virtually every member of UDT-11 and UDT-12 was given the opportunity to become airborne qualified.

The Fort Benning option was not ideal, as the wait for quotas was long and the class was time-consuming. SEAL Team One's leadership considered the Navy's parachute training facility Naval Air Station, Lakehurst, New Jersey, which offered a course significantly shorter in duration, and sent a team there to qualify and evaluate the course. It turned out to be only training for parachute riggers. Riggers had to make just one parachute jump to get the feeling of how the parachute performs so that when they rigged the things and folded them up, they would know what it was all about.

A UDT jumper wearing a football helmet, reserve and main parachute, and inflatable boat secured to his this chest, briefed in 1966 to Admiral D.L. MacDonnell, Chief of Naval Operations, by LCDR Norm Olson, Commanding Officer, UDT-11.

The team was very disappointed, and it was concluded that the Lakehurst option was not going to work. All follow-on basic parachute training left no option except reverting to the Army Airborne School. Once fully qualified in basic parachuting, West Coast UDT operators acquired the majority of their HALO training and qualifications at the Army's Yuma Test Facility in Arizona.

The only reason parachuting on the Teams evolved to the degree that it did, and the only reason the UDTs had guys ready to become SEALs, was due to the personal initiative of the early jumpers. They went out and jumped on their own time, with their own equipment, using their own money. Many became truly excellent at the sport, made personal connections in the jumping community, and developed innovations and expertise on parachute demonstration teams. When the SEAL Teams became operational, the men had the experience and expertise, and were able to then develop the tactics and capabilities needed.

# CHAPTER 9

# FREEFALL PARACHUTING IN THE TEAMS

Freefall parachuting, also referred to as "skydiving" or "sport parachuting," is the art of exiting from an aircraft at a high altitude, stabilizing the body during a delayed fall, executing various maneuvers, safely opening the parachute at a given time over a given ground reference point, and guiding the parachute so as to land on a specific target. With today's technology, training, and expertise, this art form has exceeded the wildest expectations of the early UDT-SEAL pioneers. And, no one does it better than today's U.S. Navy SEALs operationally, and by the Navy Parachute Team Leap Frogs, which exhibit their exceptional skills through public demonstrations throughout the country.

## Skydiving in the Teams — How it All Began

In 1958, DM1 Lenny Waugh from UDT-22, a graduate of the U.S. Army Basic Airborne Course, bought a parachute from Paul Grimes that he had ordered from an ad in the back of *Mechanix Illustrated* magazine. Jim McGee, also a UDT frogman and qualified military parachutist, owned and piloted a two seat Aeronca Chief airplane. One day McGee took Lenny up to jump from his airplane. As Lenny recalled: "We didn't know anything about skydiving. I read a book, and it says to jump out of an airplane, you go like this, with a picture to show you how to hold yourself in the air. That

A vintage Aeronca Chief like the one owned by Jim McGee in the 1950s.

was it. McGee took me up to 1,500 feet, which seemed like a good height to me. I didn't know how to spot or anything. I told McGee it looked good and jumped."

EM2 Frank Moncrief and Jim McGee had attended Jump School together, and Frank tells this story: "My friend McGee said, 'Frank, guess what I did this weekend.' I said, 'What was that?' And he said, 'Waugh jumped out of my airplane.' McGee took me to his car, opened the trunk, and showed me Waugh's orange and white canopy. I said, 'Where did you get that thing?' And, he said, 'The *Mechanix Illustrated* magazine.' Moncrief laughed and said, 'Maggie (McGee's nickname on the Teams), I can get a lot of those things for free from salvage.' When word got out in the Teams about this newfound joy, there was a run on the Naval Air Station's salvage depot to pick up anything that resembled a parachute." Of course the parachutes were old and past their expiration date, but as Moncrief recalled: "We didn't know any better. Those parachutes were like our babies."

Lieutenant Junior Grade Bruce Welch, another UDT friend and pilot, and Lenny Waugh alternated flying Grimes's plane and jumping. They were eventually joined by others from UDT-21 and UDT-22, including: Boitnott, Gallagher, Heinlein, Janecka, Moncrief, Tipton, Nutting, Williams, and Wilson. They comprised the nucleus of what was to become the South Norfolk Parachute Club and, unknown to them at the time, a test bed for Navy commando air capabilities development. There was no such thing as skydiving in Tidewater Virginia until these UDT men got it started.

Vintage Piper J-3 Cub.

It was pretty clear from the outset that McGee's Aeronca Chief wasn't much good for jumping. It was very small and the right door couldn't be removed, making it very difficult to exit the plane. Because of this problem, few attempts were made to effectively use it as a suitable jump platform.

A fellow named Don Wilson owned the South Norfolk Airport and was also a parachute rigger. He showed the UDT men several new things they could accomplish. In turn, the UDT men were good for Don's business, because they were bringing out new people to South Norfolk. Don was also making money from the eager UDT men. He would take them up in his Piper J-3 Cub airplane for three dollars a jump. The Piper Cub was not a good airplane for jumping, because its

Vintage Cesna-170.

slow rate of accent and limited altitude made for a long ride to jump altitude. For neophyte UDT skydivers, however, it was a challenge to be on the leading edge of the new found sport. Eventually, a Cessna-170 was obtained at South Norfolk that could hold three jumpers. It was obviously more to the liking of the parachutists, since it also had a much faster capability of getting to altitude. To expedite exits, the right door was removed and a small step was installed on the right wing strut above the wheel well.

With time, the men were able to procure and assemble harnesses, B-11 back packs, QAC chest packs, and 28-foot orange and white canopies from various military surplus salvage yards. They purchased carpenters coveralls, scrounged football helmets (cast off by a high school team nearby), and added motorcycle goggles and gloves to round out the ensemble. Stopwatches were acquired to count the estimated seconds required before deploying the main parachute after the men exited the airplanes, because they couldn't afford altimeters. Some of us personalized our canopies, dyeing them various colors without consideration for the damage it was doing to the fabric, one of many unknown hazards we were utterly unaware of at the time.

The salvage parachutes were always problematic because, they simply weren't designed for skydiving, but rather for pilots and their crewmen to escape a damaged airplane. Moreover, the men knew that they also needed a reserve parachute, so they scavenged some from those previously worn by Army aviation reserve personnel. The men had no idea of how to put them together, so they simply strapped on the Army pilot B-12 harness on their backs and the crew's QAC chest-pack harnesses on their front. It was truly a miracle they all survived. Frank Moncrief later explained: "We weren't too smart in those days. We didn't know much about skydiving at the time, but we knew we could fall out of an airplane."

Contact in the air was normally not by design, opening shocks without deployment sleeves were something to behold, and directional control of un-modified canopies were totally dependent upon wind direction and speed. Sometimes two harnesses had to be worn; one for the chest mounted reserve and the other for the main parachute.

Staff Sergeant Jim Arender of the Army Special Forces.

# LEONARD WAUGH'S RECOLLECTIONS
## LEARNING
## FROM ARMY SPECIAL FORCES

SEAL operator Lenny Waugh was an early pioneer involving parachuting in the UDT and SEAL Teams. He was a leader in developing freefall parachuting. In this photograph, Waugh is seen in Vietnam in early 1962, when he was among the first SEALs deployed to train and assist South Vietnamese naval personnel.

I heard about the innovative ways of parachuting developed by the 77th Special Forces Group on Fort Bragg. We had been down there for jumpmaster school with the 82nd Airborne Division. I got four or five jumps out of a C-130. While I was there, I learned they had a jump club like we had. So that is what gave me the idea to go down on my own time to Fort Bragg one weekend.

I was jumping for sport at the time, and I was single, so I could take trips easily. I just took it upon myself to go. I wanted to learn to freefall and that is what the Army Special Forces guys were doing.

To my mind, freefalling was going to be more useful to our UDTs. With static line, you could just throw a bag of potatoes out there, and they will land safely. You just shuffle out, hang there and the chute opens for you. If you run into any problems, like there is a backlog of jumpers or your chute malfunctions, you don't have much air left to fix it. I saw freefalling as having certain capabilities, and the flexibility to jump out of different kinds of aircraft, and that was what we needed. Now, of course, it's the only way to go.

Down in Fort Bragg, I met Jim Arender, Ron Brown, and some of the other skydivers. They took me under their wings. Over time, we formed good friendships. Several of us went down and jumped with them.

We invited them to come up and jump with our club at Oceana, and they straightened us out quite a bit. Jim Arender was among them, and he really taught us how to skydive. None of us really knew what we were doing. When we were going up, he told us: "When I go out of this airplane, I am going to turn right, then left, then do a back loop." Turning to me, he said, "What are you going to do?" I said, "I never plan." I had never thought to do so. When we jumped back then, we just jumped!

# FRANK MONCRIEF'S JIM ARENDER STORY

## "WE THOUGHT HE WAS GOING TO DIE"

UDT operator Frank Moncrief tells a similar Jim Arender story: "He was one hell of a guy, and everyone knew about him. One weekend, Lenny Waugh brought him up to our drop zone at the South Norfolk airport. It had two grass runways. Jim looked around, and said, "Where's the DZ?" Now, he's used to jumping down in Fort Bragg, where they have models of the town of Ste. Mere Eglise (France) and Eindhoven (Netherlands) as practice drop zones that are ten miles long and five miles wide. Ours was just two dirt runways.

When Jim got ready to jump, he said, "Okay, guys. I am going to go to altitude and I am going to jump, and I am going to make a 360 right and a 360 left, a back loop then I am going to pull my rip cord." And he did just that.

Frank Moncrief with Jim Tipton circa 1962.

We used to do same things, but we didn't tell anybody what we were going to do in advance, because we really didn't know what we're going to do when we stepped out of the plane. While we did all of those things, but actually it was called uncontrolled jumping.

Jim Arender pulled his ripcord, just like he said he would. We all watched in horror as a piece of his parachute flew off and there was a big hole in the back of it. "Oh, my God," I said. "Something's not right." We thought he was going to die.

But then Arender steered that parachute down and around just as nice as you could imagine, and landed light as a feather. We rushed over to him and said, "Jim! What was that? What happened to your parachute?"

Arender was puzzled by our concern. Then he realized what we were talking about and laughed, saying, "Oh, that was my sleeve." We said, "What is a sleeve?" And, he says, "When you pull that down over a parachute, it will slow down your opening." We all looked at each other. "But you've got a hole—a big hole in your parachute." "No, that's not a hole." He said. "That's how I steer."

## Learning from Army Special Forces

To learn more about skydiving, Lenny Waugh went to Fort Bragg to contact an Army Special Forces friend who was on the XVIII Airborne Corps, Strategic Army Corps Parachute Team, later to become the Army Parachute Team—Golden Knights. Staff Sergeant Jim Arender was considered a pioneering skydiver, who, in 1960, was the first U.S. citizen to win a gold medal at a World Skydiving Championships. Two years later, he was the first American to become the overall world champion.

Learning from Army Special Forces allowed the UDT men to make quantum strides in perfecting their skydiving skills, which ultimately allowed them to excel, develop, and refine military tactics, techniques, and procedures using High-Altitude, Low-Opening (HALO) parachute capabilities.

The UDT men had a lot to learn about skydiving. Jim did a series of demonstration jumps during a visit to Norfok. When he came back down to earth, he found the UDT men were full of questions. First they asked about the piece of the parachute that seemed to fly off when he opened his canopy. Jim explained what they were seeing was the parachute sleeve. Using such a sleeve would slow the opening of the parachute, eliminating those jarring openings that had resulted in many bloody jumpsuits. Jim Arender showed the men how to fold the parachute and and then to slide the sleeve over it. After pulling the ripcord, the chute slides out of the sleeve before it fully opens, which slows down the opening.

The UDT men were equally excited about how Jim could plan and control his freefall and his landing. This was big stuff. Arender explained how it was possible: "You go five feet up from the skirt, cut the material out on gore 28, and then tape it. That gives you the ability to steer. If you pull your riser down on the right, it'll turn right. If you pull on left, it will go left—see, you've got steer-ability."

The men were pretty excited about this newly discovered information, and instead of heading out to hit the town, they spent the night in the airport hangar modifying parachutes. Just as Jim Arender instructed, the men cut their chutes and taped

The men modified old T-10 parachutes by cutting out part of the gore panels in the back. This picture shows a newly steerable salvaged parachute with which the men practiced water jumps. Note the fins on this man's feet.

the edges up—with masking tape. Masking tape, however, was a bad idea, since it did not have enough adhesive strength to keep the fabric from ripping apart where it was cut. No one mentioned sewing tape, thus it's a wonder they all survived. Later, one of the early UDT jumpers, Bill Bruhmuller, had the brilliant idea of using a soldering iron to cut through the nylon. The soldering iron would melt closed the nylon fabric that was being cut, eliminating the need for sewing tape or for frogmen to do the sewing. The edges held together pretty well for a half dozen jumps.

The Norfolk Club eventually became affiliated with the Parachute Club of America (PCA), which is now the United States Parachute Association (USPA). The USPA has four levels of license, with (D) requiring 200 qualification jumps. As noted above, many of the pioneering frogmen attained D-licenses in the early 1960s, which is significant, considering that 55-plus years later, the number of D-licenses exceeds 36,000, and nearly 200 Association Members have been awarded "Jump Wings" for achieving 8,000 jumps. The license numbering system is chronological and tells its own story: Waugh (D-128), Nutting (D-131), Janecka (D-460), Moncrief (D-519) and Heinlein (D-708).

Three UDT men sweep all events in a central Florida competition: (l-r) Frank Moncrief, Wayne Boles, and Lenny Waugh.

"Freedom of freefall, the peacefulness of the parachute ride, the camaraderie that lasts a lifetime...from start to finish, this is what brings a diverse cross-section of individuals together. It is our shared passion," Andy Keech, quoted in his book *Skies Call*.

Separately, Stan Janecka, an operator from UDT-21, went on to garner prominence in national competition as a style and accuracy competitor. In 1960, fewer than 12 baton passes had been completed in freefall between two skydivers. In March, at the South Norfolk Airport, Lenny Waugh and Stewart Whisman exited the

UDT operators demonstrating a baton pass while freefalling. The orange smoke containers on their ankles allow spectators on the ground to better observe the parachutist.

# AIRCRAFT USED FOR HIGH ALTITUDE JUMPS

SEAL Military Free Fall missions required the use of U.S. Navy aircraft to jump at altitudes requiring supplemental oxygen. In response, the Naval Air Force (NAVAIR) provided three aircraft:

The A3-D Skywarrior was a carrier-based strategic (jet-powered) bomber, which could climb to 40,000 feet and open the nose wheel, providing the capability for six jumpers to exit by sliding down a chute. Since the pilots had never witnessed live exits, it gave them confidence that it could be done during an aircraft emergency.

The P2-V Neptune was a land-based, long-range maritime patrol and anti-submarine warfare propeller-driven aircraft. This plane was capable of delivering eight jumpers from a belly hatch in the tail.

The C1-A Trader was a U.S. Navy carrier onboard delivery (COD) aircraft used to ferrying personnel and supplies to ships on station at sea. This airplane was capable of delivering eight jumpers from its side door, and was used early on to demonstrate that the SEALs could effectively and confidently carryout the air requirements of their mission.

plane at 7,000 feet and successfully passed the 13th baton at 5,000 feet. In a three-man team competition in Central Florida, Wayne Boles, Frank Moncrief, and Lenny Waugh swept all events, garnering separate and overall trophies.

Owing to the prohibitive cost of making civilian parachute jumps, the Norfolk Club's UDT men approached the commanding officer at the Oceana Naval Air Station in Virginia Beach, Virginia through the operations officer. Their goal was to obtain permission to conduct parachute operations on the base. The commander tentatively approved the request, pending the outcome of a demonstration of their skydiving skills. Nutting, Waugh, Wilson, and Moncrief dazzled the commanding officer. He supported formation of the Tidewater Navy Parachute Club, and provided a building for them to use as a parachute loft. He also made available a Navy Flying Club twin-engine Beech Craft, which could carry four jumpers, and the opportunity to schedule pilots on a not-to-interfere basis.

## Early Experimentation with HALO Jumps

In the early 1960s, Army Special Forces began formal Military Free Fall (MFF) parachute instruction in Fort Bragg, NC. High Altitude - Low Opening (HALO) parachuting is a military concept to airdrop personnel at high altitudes when aircraft are unable to fly above hostile skies without posing a threat to the jumpers. In a typical HALO jump, the parachutist will exit from the aircraft, free-fall from altitudes between 18,000 and 35,000 feet, outfitted with supplemental oxygen. After falling for a period of time at terminal velocity, the operator opens his parachute at a low altitude.

During a HALO jump, men can position their bodies to reach speeds of 180 mph. This is accomplished by adopting a somewhat rigid posture; with legs straightened and arms tucked close to the body. This allows jumpers to "track" or maneuver through the air. Because jumpers are so small and have little forward airspeed, they are hard to detect on radar. Moreover, the chute is open for a relatively short period of time, thus, there is less chance the jumper will be seen. The men liked the idea of HALO jumping because it provided a stealthy way to get to potential targets.

An early picture of a UDT HALO jumper using oxygen to breath at high altitude during free fall.

The technique of High Altitude-High Opening (HAHO)—discussed below—was also developed as a tactic to infiltrate SEALs by opening parachutes at high altitude and gliding for several miles off-set from the target location. Both are known as Military Free Fall techniques.

Military Free Fall (MFF) was derived from sport parachuting from the late 1950s onward. U.S. Special Operations Forces, including U.S. Navy SEALs, began formal MFF insertions using the "Rogallo Wing," (parawing) designed by Francis Rogallo, which could be controlled very much like a glider. This parachute was primarily used in sport parachuting during the 1970's. The parawing was replaced by the "parafoil," first invented in the middle 1960's by Domina Jalbert, a kite maker. The parafoil or ram-air parachute is a deformable airfoil that maintains its profile by trapping air between two rectangular- shaped membranes, sewn together at the trailing edge and sides, but open at the leading edge.

Within the military, only Special Operations Forces conduct Military Free Fall operations and this, of course, includes SEALs. The men of UDT began freefall parachuting on their own time and with their own equipment at civilian airports. Some trained with Army Special Forces, and many of these men were among the first SEALs.

First HALO Class from SEAL Team TWO. Back Row: LTJG Macione, LTJG DiMartino, TM1 Janecka, TM1 Tipton, BM1 Kusinski, SM1 Wallace, BM3 Finley. Kneeling: SK1 Goinse, DM1 Waugh, SN McKeon, AT2 Brozac, HM1 McCarty.

When the SEAL Teams were formed in January 1962, the East Coast men continued to go to Fort Bragg, North Carolina for parachute jumping, while the West Coast men went to the Marine Corps Air Station, Yuma, Arizona. It was a continuation of the horse trading that the UDT men always had to do; trading HALO jumping for training in SCUBA, foreign weapons, and kitchen demolitions (making explosives from things found in the kitchen and elsewhere around the home).

In view of the proximity to Fort Bragg and the long-standing relationship that the UDTs, and later the SEALs had with Army Special Forces, we were able to arrange for the first cadre of twelve SEALs to attend Army Special Forces HALO Training.

Because the SEALs had a wealth of freefall experience, the ground training was minimal and they started immediately at 18,000 feet; progressing to 40,000 feet. Learning how to handle the oxygen bottle was also a brief matter, because maintaining complex closed-circuit SCUBA was commonplace. However, pre-breathing 100% oxygen while, climbing to altitude is necessary in order to flush nitrogen from the bloodstream.

SEAL MFF trainees also had to learn how to deal with temperature extremes around 25 to 35 degrees below zero at 30,000 feet. The bright side, however, is that when descending, the atmosphere drops three degrees per thousand feet. The technique was to unzip and peel off layers as you fall, but that's easier said than done.

At 40,000 feet, the air is thin and the jumpers have a fall-rate of about 250 mph. As they descend to about 15,000 feet, they reach terminal velocity of 120 mph and control their descent to the opening altitude at about 4,000 feet. The jumpers have to learn how to control their movements in the air, so that they land in a group in a designated area. Jumping at night with combat equipment is a challenge. As time passed, more SEALs were trained in HALO, and overall, they attained excellence in their "Air" capability by using a combination of specialized training, equipment, and tactics.

When the SEALs jumped, they realized that they would have to wait to slow down the terminal velocity zone. If you've ever put your

An early SEAL HALO jumper using oxygen to breathe at high altitudes during freefall.

A SEAL Team operator seen making an equipment jump with a current-day HAHO rig.

hand out the window of a fast-moving car, you've probably experienced it going up and down. When you jump at high altitude from a very fast a plane, your whole body goes like that. If you put your hand out just a little bit, it will spin you like crazy. So the men had to learn to wait until they slowed down to control their movements. Other areas developed were techniques for grouping in the air, jumping with combat equipment, and night descents. In all cases, accuracy was important; you have to be able to land where you want to land.

By the early 1980s, SEALs had developed a HAHO capability, where opening the parachute seconds after exiting the aircraft allows for longer travel distance due to increased canopy time and allowing travelling distances of more than 30 or more miles, depending on exit altitude. Jumpers will use a compass or GPS device for guidance while flying, and use terrain features to navigate to their desired landing zone. When deploying as a team, they form up in a stack while airborne under canopy.

# A SOF HALO PIONEER

## WILFRED "SQUEAK" CHARETTE

### November 14, 1936 - May 9, 2010

Wilfred "Squeak" Charette was a former Special Forces Non-Commissioned Officer and CIA officer whose last duty station was as the CIA's Liaison Officer to the Special Operatios Command until he retired in 1996. He passed away in 2010.

Charette was a pioneer in development of the High-Altitude, Low-Opening (HALO) parachute capability for the Special Operations Forces community. (His got his nickname, "Squeak" because his Corcoran jump boots squeaked when he walked.)

In the summer of 1963, along with the rest of the HALO Committee, he trained the first HALO class from SEAL Team TWO. The Navy provided the aircraft for this training based on what it thought might be available for SEAL operations. The A3D Skywarrior strategic bomber was used because it was aircraft carrier-capable as well as its high speed and altitude. Other aircraft included the P2V Neptune anti-submarine aircraft, which was used for its long-distance ability; the S2F Tracker; and the C-130 Hercules. The SEALs and the HALO Committee made jumps from the A3D at 40,000 feet with a parachute opening altitude of 4,000 feet.

The A3D reportedly flew at 220 mph when the men exited the aircraft, and it took several jumps of trial and error for the men to develop good procedures and body position given the high speed and thin air. During these jumps the men experienced sub-zero temperatures when they left the aircraft and in free fall, but after the parachute opened at 4,000 feet, they had to strip off gloves and unzip protective clothing as they descended to avoid heat stroke in the 80 to 90 degree weather on the ground. The thin air at 40,000 feet also caused their terminal velocity to be faster for much of the jump. One

Wil "Squeak" Charette was one of the original members of the US Army Parachute Team.

Wil Charettte in an undated photograph taken in Laos while working for the CIA.

of the SEALs recalled, however, that they still experienced more than three minutes of freefall before the chute opened at 4,000 feet.

During this training Charette asked two experienced SEAL jumpers, Lenny Waugh and Stan Janecka, to participate in a HALO demonstration jump for a general officer to showcase that the HALO Committee also trained the other services. Charette told the SEALs to land as close to the general as possible. Janecka took that literally, and the general had to duck to avoid being hit as Janecka landed next to him. A few months after those 40,000 foot jumps with the SEALs, Charette took a team of Army and Air Force jumpers to California and, in December 1963, conducted a record 43,500 foot HALO jump from a C-130.

Wil "Squeak" Charette made many contributions to furthering man's knowledge on HALO parachuting, and today's significant SOF HALO insertion capability can be attributed to his efforts and those of the other early Army and Navy HALO pioneers.

# CHAPTER 10

# PARACHUTE DEMONSTRATION TEAMS

## Original U.S. Navy Parachute Demonstration Team—Chuting Stars

When the U.S. Navy's Chuting Stars parachute demonstration team was originally established, they formed a long-standing professional relationship with the U.S. Army's Golden Knights parachute demonstration team. The "Knights" were established in early 1960, but they didn't become the official U.S. Army Parachute Team until later that year.

The original "Stars" were formed at the Naval Air Facility (NAF), El Centro, California in 1961, which was the 50th anniversary of Naval Aviation. They were only scheduled to operate for one year, but the demand for their performances remained very high, and as a result, in 1962, the team moved to what was hoped to be a permanent home at Naval Air Station (NAS) Pensacola, Florida.

The first men assigned to the origial team were all volunteers taken from the fleet and Naval Test Parachute Unit at El Centro. Several men from the UDTs volunteered for

Official Chuting Stars jump aircraft C-117D.

73

The circa 1961 original Oceana demo team members jumped in their personal equipment with no uniformity.

Briefing before a demonstration jump.

this assignment, but only Frank Moncrief of UDT-22 was selected. He remained with the Chuting Stars through the first show season, however, when SEAL Team TWO was established in 1962, he was anxious to get back to his Teammates and return to Little Creek for duty. Frank was my classmate in East Coast UDT Training Class

"Stars" exiting from the team aircraft.

"Stars" flying in tandem with smoke.

5, and one of the initial 15 frogmen selected to attend, with me, the U.S. Army's Basic Airborne Course —Class 14, Fort Benning, Georgia in 1956.

Unfortunately, two years later, in 1964, the team was disbanded because the money dried up. Yet, in 1969, the Chuting Stars were reconstituted again at the Naval Air Technical Training Center (NATTC), Lakehurst, New Jersey. Over the next several years, the team never got strong the support it needed from "Navy-Air," and was disbanded for good in 1971. Perhaps the team could have continued on, but the men would have had to beg, borrow, and steal for equipment and aircraft support.

When the Chuting Stars got disbanded at Lakehurst, team jumpers Photographer's Mate "Chip" Maury and Parachute Rigger Al Schmiz were available for transfer. Through liaisons established with Chief Gene Gagliardi, and member of the UDT Para-Team (West) at in Coronado, California, and subsequently me as UDT-11's commanding officer, we worked with the Navy to get both men assigned UDT-11 and the UDT Para-Team. "Chip" Maury was one of the premier aerial photographers of his day; Al Schmiz was a superb skydiver with a wealth of demonstration experience. Both

Frank Moncrief, a UDT-SEAL operator, was a member of the Chutuing Stars during its first season.

went on to contribute greatly during the burgeoning growth of Naval Special Warfare's introduction to the parachute demonstration world.

Regrettably, "Navy Air" never recognized the contributions of the Chuting Stars sailors. To remedy this oversight, a large plaque with photos and rosters of all the personnel that had ever been assigned to the team was constructed for display purposes. In the view of many, the natural location

Chip Morey ( left ) and Al Schmiz (right)were members of the Chuting Stars for the first and second show seasons.

for this plaque should have been the Naval Aviation Museum in Pensacola, Florida, but the museum staff decided that the team, a once nationally recognized organization, did not meet their requirements for permanent display.

Over time, the Chuting Stars jumpers had lost contact and personal relationships with the Army's Golden Knights Parachute Team. Recently, however, some visited the magnificent headquarters and training facilities at Fort Bragg, North Carolina. The men observed and suggested that perhaps Fort Bragg would be a far better location for the plaque to reside, as a place where the history of the Navy Parachute Jump Team would be known and appreciated. Contact was made, and the "Knights," welcomed the "Stars" into their fold, for indeed, they were "comrades in arms." The Navy Parachute Team had at long last received recognition, and by the worlds greatest parachute organization, no less. The efforts to attain proper recognition had been long and arduous process with a number of difficulties to overcome. Many of the "Stars" are no longer with us, and the survivors are now elderly men and no longer "Sailors afloat on a Sea of Air."

While the original Chuting Stars were in existence off and on for only 10 years, their professional reputation was held in high esteem by the Navy, the general public, and particularly the Army Golden Knights. And, while they were not involved directly with Naval Special Warfare, their indirect lineage had a positive effect on the initial formation of the West and East UDT Para-Teams and follow-on jump teams.

Plaque commemorating the U.S. Navy Parachute Team Chuting Stars, which is on display at the headquarters of the U.S. Army's Golden Knights in Fort Bragg, North Carolina.

## Original UDT Para-Team (West)—Leap Frogs

In November 1963, at the rank of Lieutenant Commander, I was reassigned to the West Coast as the Commanding Officer of UDT-11. As one of the early East Coast jumpers, I was eager to meet Chief Gene Gagliardi. He introduced me to the local jumping elite, and I immediately got caught up in the euphoria of their advanced expertise. I slowly became accepted as a mainstay in the San Diego Skydivers, one of the nation's first sports parachuting clubs.

Subsequently, at the goading of Chief Gagliardi, I recommended to my boss, Commander Naval Operations Support Group, PACIFIC that consideration be given to creating a small demonstration team

Original UDT West Coast UDT Para-Team: Storekeeper (SK2) Donald "Herky" Hertenstein, Chief Photographer's Mate (PHC) Gene Gagliardi, LCDR Norm Olson, Photographer's Mate (PH2) Donald P. "Chip" Maury, and Parachute Rigger First Class (PR1) Al Schmiz, circa 1955.

comprised of a cadre of highly qualified skydivers. He accepted my recommdation.

The team initially consisted of five jumpers: LCDR Olson, Chief Photographer's Mate (PHC) Gagliardi, Storekeeper (SK2) "Herky" Hertenstein, Parachute Rigger First Class (PR1) Al Schmiz, and Photographer's Mate Second Class (PH2) Donald P. "Chip" Maury. Schmiz and Maury were members of the Navy's original Chuting Stars.

Operations were to be conducted on a not-to-interfere basis with other military duties and at no cost to the government, other than using normally scheduled aircraft. In fact, the majority of the team's training jumps were conducted at private airports, and at the jumpers own expense.

At the outset, we used our personally owned parachutes and equipment, which provided little uniformity, no matter how well the jumps were executed. To overcome this dilemma, and still remain within the "no cost to the government" provision, unique procurement techniques were employed. There is an old saying in the Navy: If you

Para-Commander—The most innovation parachute design in 35 years.

Chief Gagliardi getting a rigger's check by the jumpmaster before boarding the support helicopter.

Norm Olson in freefall over Southern California.

Para-Team preparing for a demonstration jump.

U.S. Navy Parachute Exhibition Team.

Olson briefing the team before a demonstration.

Naval Aviation News Magazine features a photograph of LCDR Olson re-enlisting PH2 Chip Maury.

August 1965 cover of Sky Diver Magazine taken by PH2 Chip Maury.

This picture of the team exiting a Navy HW-26 appeared in Sky Diver Magazine.

need something, ask a chief (the Navy's top enlisted man). Chiefs get things done. Chief Gagliardi went out and worked some magic, coming back with Pioneer jumpsuits embroidered in Tijuana, he said. That wasn't all. He had Bell helmets, French jump boots, altimeters, and white and blue state-of-the-art parachutes. Para-Commander parachute canopies, which represented the most radical canopy design in 35 years, elevated the capability and status of the team significantly. In all, Chief Gagliardi procured hundreds of dollars' worth of equipment back when hundreds of dollars was real money. We were a team and finally looked the part. To this day, I have no idea how he did it, and I had the sense never to ask.

The original Leap Frogs logo recognized members from the UDT and SEAL Teams and the Beach Jumper Unit (BJU), a cover and deception organization that became a part of Naval Special Warfare during the Vietnam period.

A short time later, the original logo was replaced with this short-lived, but more tranditional emblem identifying "Naval Special Warfare Group ONE" as the parent command.

The emblem that includes the Navy SEAL Trident and Freddy the Frog under a U.S. Navy canopy was adopted thereafter, and has stood the test of time for over 50 years.

Following a jump, Captain Phil Bucklew (center) introduced LCDR Norm Olson to Admiral Thomas Morrer, Commander U.S. Pacific Fleet. Admiral Morrer went on to become the Chief of Naval Operations and Chairman of the Joint Chiefs of Staff.

Chip Maury presenting Gene Gagliardi his USPA Gold Wings during his 1,000th jump.

The Team's initial purpose was to visually enhance the many local UDT demonstrations, both on base and off. The concept was approved in January 1964 and met with immediate success, not only in helping to tell the UDT story, but that of the overall Navy. As time went on, the UDT Parachute Team's reputation gained popularity and requests for locally sponsored weekend demonstrations spread throughout California and Arizona. During this embryonic stage of development, the team in 1965 received notoriety by appearing on the cover of *Sky Diver Magazine* and *Navy Aviation News*.

The West Coast Leap Frogs circa 1970's launched from the tail ramp of a C-130 already in this formation.

Having helped to set the stage in 1964 for the birth of the UDT Para-Team, I became impressed over time with the dedication and professionalism of the initial cadre of frogmen. As the team matured and the talent of the skydivers grew exponentially, the adoption of the name Leap Frogs elevated the team to national status and the integration of the key component of Naval Special Warfare Group ONE.

PHCS Gene Gagliardi, jump master for the team, said: "The name needed some changing—something catchy! One day when the team was all together the name 'Leap Frogs' came up and stuck." Since the team is made up of UDT and SEAL Team members who are U.S. Navy "frogmen," the name Leap Frogs has particular significance.

On July 4th, 1969, the Navy's only exhibition parachute team made its debut as the Leap Frogs at Coronado's annual celebration. Formerly, the team was known as the U. S. Navy UDT/SEAL Exhibition Parachute Team.

The "Leap Frogs" with Warrant Officer Wayne Boles as officer-in-charge, consisted of free-fall parachutists from the Underwater Demolition Teams and the SEAL Teams home based at the U. S. Naval Amphibious Base, Coronado.

## Original UDT Para-Team (East)—Chuting Stars

While the West Coast was on the leading edge of Navy demonstration jumping, the East Coast was not progressing significantly in this realm, though they had a very active sport parachuting club sponsored by Naval Air Station Oceana, Virginia.

On the East Coast, the jumper's most significant relationship resided in the close personal and professional contact they had with Fort Bragg, the cradle of Army parachuting and the home of the Golden Knights. As a result, they were exposed to the latest innovations in parachute design and function. They were able to incorporate these capabilities in their personal skydiving activities, and in the tactical employment of the operational UDT-SEAL Teams.

Jumpmaster Moncrief spotting the exit point.

Commander Olson following orders.

# Danang Republic of Vietnam

U.S. Naval Advisory Detachment (USNAD) and Joint Operational Advisory Team: Navy SEALs, Force Recon Marines, and Navy Special Boat Support Unit personnel. CDR Olson is standing far left.

During my tour as Commanding Officer, UDT-11, I deployed several times to Southeast Asia and Vietnam on combat operations. Following this tour, I was promoted to Commander and assigned to the U.S. Military Assistance Command, Vietnam-Studies and Observations Group, (USMACV-SOG), as Commanding Officer, U.S. Naval Advisory Detachment (USNAD). During this assignment, I made 19 military freefall jumps from a variety of SOG Aircraft; qualifying as a Master Parachutist with the airborne units of the Republics of South Vietnam and Thailand.

Following my tour as Commanding Officer of UDT-11 and Commander Maritime Operations Group, USMACV-SOG, I was transferred back to the East Coast as Chief Staff Officer, Naval Special Warfare Group ATLANTIC (now Naval Special Warfare Group TWO) in 1968. I immediately returned to freefall parachuting at the Oceana Parachute Club and the civilian drop zone in Suffolk, Virginia, where the majority of the East Coast jumpers earned their skydiving stripes.

Riggers check before boarding the Navy DC-3.

It was clear to me that a formally endorsed Navy parachute team was not happenning on the East Coast, and that it would be up to me to do something about it. In early 1969, a group of eight officers and 23 enlisted men from UDT-21, UDT-22, and SEAL Team TWO, were highly motivation to develop a parachute demonstration team, and I was one of them. I had the experience from the West Coast, and fortunately, I was in a position of authority so that Icould make it happen. Once again, I presented the case to my boss, and it was endorsed heartily. As a result, we tailored the Para-Team East much like its predecessor on the West Coast.

The skill of the skydivers was not in question, but the biggest hurdle was convincing the leadership that the operations would be conducted on a not-too-interfere basis with other military duties, and that "there would be no cost to the government," other than using normally scheduled aircraft.

Main and reserve parachute and helmet and altimeter typically worn by the demonstration team jumpers.

Fortuitously, my immediate superior was Commader, Naval Special Warfare Group TWO. He had also been the senior officer on the West Coast that approved creation of that parachute demonstration team. He was impressed with the growth of the Leap Frogs and, as a result, gave us the go-ahead, subject to the same limitations mentioned above.

The black jumpsuits, white Bell helmets, French jump boots and the red, white and blue Para-Commander parachute canopies made a statement at the time, as did the black and white logo design, which was a likeness of the San Diego Sky Divers logo. As time went on, the team changed colors to blue and gold, with the same logo design. As the team grew in stature and represented

Naval Special Warfare Group TWO team before one of their many demonstrations.

The UDT-SEAL Para-Team ALANTIC became the Navy Parachute Team EAST.

UDT-SEAL Para Team ATLANTIC, circa 1973: Standing: Dave Blagoue, Tom Morris, Jim Davis, Bill Curtis, Ed Leisure, and Pierre Ponson. Kneeling: Dave Sutherland, Norm Carley, UKN, Tim Slatterly, Dan Zmuda, and Billy Acklin.

The SEAL-UDT Atlantic Parachute Team adopted the Leap Frog's logo design and resurrected the Chuting Stars team name.

JULY 1979

Back row, (l-r): WD Powers, Herschel Davis, Al Horner, Joe Hulse, Bob Pelt, Frank Moncrief, Bo Burwell. Front row: Doug Ellis, Pierre Ponson, Ty Zellers, John Porter, Dan Zmuda. Note that Ty Zellers is jokingly wearing the jump suit of LT Rick Wollard.

# LEAPFROGS MEET JUMPING LEGEND

## STORY AND PHOTOS BY: JOC (SCW) ROBERT FEINBERG, PUBLIC AFFAIRS OFFICER, NAVY PARACHUTE TEAM

The members of the San Diego based Navy Parachute Team (NPT), recently met and went skydiving with a true legend of jumping, Capt. (SEAL) (RET) Norm Olson. [Editor's Note: Olson founded the Navy Parachute Team in 1964 and served as its Officer in Charge for four years. Two years later the team made its debut as the "Leapfrogs." Subsequently, the team was sanctioned by the Department of Defense and established in 1974 as the U.S. Navy Parachute Demonstration Team.]

Members of the NPT took some of their own time to skydive with Olson during his visit to San Diego. Olson said the following after the jumps, "It was a fantastic privilege to jump with them. I was hoping to hold my own and I faked it well."

Over the course of the several days spent with Olson, the NPT members were able to gather a lot of insight into the origins and workings of the team in the past. Olson said, "There is no comparison from the old team to the new one. For one thing, we were all assigned to the

CAPT Olson in the foreground, right, preparing to jump with the Leap Frogs.

NPT under temporary duty orders, while the new guys are all permanently assigned. We also had to beg and borrow to get aircraft for our jumps and some times to get proper equipment.

"After 21 years, so much has changed in the sport. From the jumpsuits, to the technology of the parachutes and the ability to control them has vastly improved. Also, in the air a lot of physical movements have altered to more leg/spine moves."

Engineman Chief Petty Officer (SEAL) Dave Casper, NPT aircraft scheduler, said, "I was impressed because he was a legend in the teams. He started it all and for someone in their 70's he skydives pretty well."

To make the event even more exciting for Olson, the very first jump with the team marked his 200th jump since his reentry in the sport over the past year. He has approximately 2,400 jumps during his lifetime.

Olson also noted, "Safety has improved immensely, mostly with the ability to control landings. Most of my injuries are parachute related during my time on the teams and I'd say 90 percent of them are landing related. Serving on the Leapfrogs is a great experience and I don't think a lot of the team guys realize how much time and effort goes into what we do on the NPT. I also believe the experience and knowledge gained on the jump team helped formulate what the modern day SEAL teams are taught about skydiving."

Captain Olson, in the center of the formation in a powder-blue jump suit, is seen jumping with the modern-day Leap Frogs over Southern California.

additional commands, the UDT-SEAL logo was replaced with an anchor representing the U.S. Navy.

During the 1970s, the Ram Air Parachutes, commonly referred to as the "Square", was rapidly displacing round parachutes, and the Team immediately adopted it for its versatility during training and particularly demonstrations.

The big break for the team came in 1973 during the annual Azalea Day Festival Air Show at the Naval Air Station, Norfolk, Virginia. Historically, this had been a Golden Knights performance; however, that year the Army had a scheduling conflict and had to renege. Being consummate  opportunists, the Para-Team stepped in and put on a superb performance.

A Para-Team jumper lands in front of the grandstand with a snappy salute at the Azalea Day Festival Air Show.

Unexpectedly, Rear Admiral F. H. Miller, Commander Naval Recruiting Command, was in attendance and he expressed his pleasure to my boss Rear Admiral W.M.A. Greene, Commander Naval Inshore Warfare Command, ATLANTIC. Several weeks later, as a Navy Captain, I had a personal audience in Washington with Rear Admiral Miller, who approved combining and supporting the West and East Coast demonstration teams directly under the U.S. Navy Recruiting Command as the joint Navy Parachute Demonstration Teams.

When both teams merged under the Navy Parachute Team umbrella, the East Coast adopted the Original Chuting Stars logo, and the West Coast retained the sacred name "Leap Frogs." The dividing line for scheduled demonstrations was the Mississippi River. Like on the West Coast, patch and uniform colors also evolved.

Initially there was little contact between both Teams, but as time progressed, annual joint training evolved. Members from both Navy Parachute Teams were nominated and selected to participate in Military and National Competitions, where "All Navy" and "All Military" freefall records were jointly established. In 1978, selected personnel from both Teams participated in the U.S. National Parachuting Championships at

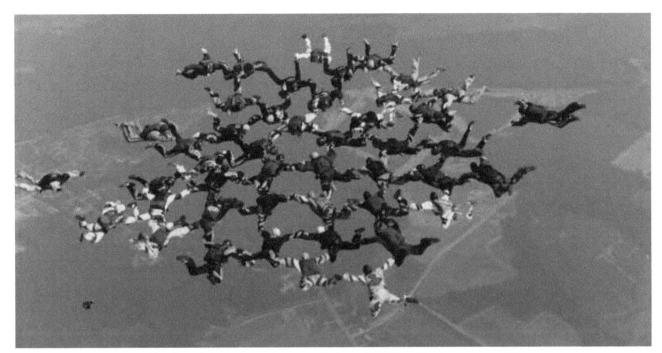

All-military 32-man formation conducted over NAS Memphis, Tennessee in 1980.

Richmond, Indiana. Then, In 1980, military skydivers gathered at the Naval Air Station, Memphis, Tennessee to participate in large formation skydive from a C-130 provided by the U.S. Air Force Reserve.

Fourteen jumps were made over a four-day period; cumulating in a successful, all-military, 32-way, record skydive. It was a combined effort by the Navy's Leap Frogs and Chuting Stars, with a sprinkling of a few other military personnel not affiliated with a formal team or club. While not significant by today's standards, this jump was made in 1980, and was quite astounding for its time.

Over the intervening years, the Chuting Stars gained national recognition east of the Mississippi by supporting Navy Recruiting and promoting the Naval Special Warfare community to the American public.

After forming and leading the Team for the initial year, I had a three year leave of absence from skydiving while I was a student the Naval War College, followed by an **obligational assignment** in the Pentagon. When I returned to the Naval Amphibious Base, Little Creek, I became involved once again with the Para-Team, participating in training jumps and demonstrations,—always on a not-to-interfere basis with my official duties.

During my 12-year affiliation with the East Coast Para-Team, turned Chuting Stars, I had an "upfront and personal" opportunity to observe the maturity and professionalism displayed by the highest skill level of demonstration skydiving.

The Chuting Stars on their final flight.

During the last three years of my 30 years of military service, I was stationed at Fort Bragg, North Carolina, the home of the Army Airborne and the Golden Knights Parachute Team. When I had free time on weekends, I was able to jump with one of the three sport parachute clubs (XVIII Airborne, 82 Airborne, and Green Beret), as well as at the nearby civilian drop zone at the Raeford Airport.

Returning to Little Creek for a final farewell, I was accompanied by three other prominent SEALs that were also retiring: Commander John Boyd, Lieutenant Commander Tom Truxell, and Lieutenant Commander Jack Macione. Following the outdoor ceremony, we were honored by the U.S. Navy Parachute Demonstration Team comprised of the Leap Frogs and Chuting Stars. This evoked a hearty "Hooyah" by all.

## Leap Frogs Today

In 1994, the 30-year history of Naval Special Warfare's involvement with the U.S. Navy Parachute Demonstration Team had literally been a series of ups and downs, primarily due to limited command support and the temporary nature of personnel assignments.

Presented to Captain Norman Olson by the Chuting Stars in 1978.

Fortunately, the capability of the team was finally accepted and institutionalized as a permanent organization within the Naval Special Warfare Command. This meant the billets for manning the team were officially authorized and funding guaranteed permanent team assignment for a three-year tour of duty.

The Chief of Naval Operations assigned to the Leap Frogs the mission of demonstrating Navy excellence through out the United States by supporting Navy recruiting efforts and promoting the Naval Special Warfare community to the American public.

Captain Norman Olson poses with the Leap Frogs in 2016.

Today the U.S. Navy Parachute Team is comprised of Navy SEALs, Special Warfare Combatant-Craft Crewmen (SWCC), and Parachute Riggers assigned to Naval Special Warfare. Each member is a volunteer and assigned for a guarateed three-year tour. They are drawn from the Naval Special Warfare Groups located on the East and West Coasts. Upon completion of their tours, members return to operational duties at a SEAL or Special Boat Team.

While the early military parachute clubs, civilian drop zones, and UDT-SEAL demonstration teams were not universally accepted by the operational teams, they provided a useful function by promoting Navy and Naval Special Warfare recruiting.

The Leap Frogs display the American flag over Chicago during a recent performance. (Photo courtesy Jim Woods)

What was lost throughout the evolution of these early pioneers was that most of their skydiving expertise was learned at the expense of the individual operators. The benefit of this experience was manifested in their exposure to the current parachute technology and the latest freefall techniques.

Through their early "Air" pioneering efforts, Navy SEALs have proudly upheld the legacy of the eagle that is represented on the SEAL breast insignia. Moreover; these latent parachuting milestones have significantly enhanced the current tactical parachuting and other air capabilities mastered by today's SEALs.

U.S. Navy Parachute Demonstration Team Leap Frogs are a special breed of warriors. Here they trail smoke in a tethered flag maneuver. (Photo courtesy Jim Woods)

# CHAPTER 11

# THE FULTON SKYHOOK AND MARITIME RECOVERY SYSTEM

The parachuting capabilities of the UDT and SEAL Teams have evolved since the early 1950s, however, other significant air capabilities progressed in the tactics, techniques, and procedures used by the UDT and later SEAL Teams; some not so successful. One was the Fulton Surface-to-Air Recovery System (STARS) used by the U.S. Air Force, Marine Corps, and Navy for retrieving equipment and personnel from the ground or water. The system was developed by the inventor Robert E. Fulton, Jr. for the Office of Naval Research with the assistance of the Marine Corps.

U.S. experimentation began in the early 1950s with the CIA and Air Force.. The system used an overall-type harness and a self-inflating helium balloon that attached to a lift line and the harness. A support aircraft engaged this line with a V-shaped yoke, and the individual was quickly yanked into the air like a sling shot and reeled aboard the aircraft. Red flags on the lift line guided the pilot during daylight recoveries; lights on the lift line were used for night recoveries. Kits were designed for one and two-man recoveries, and dropped by the recovery aircraft

Illustration of the operating principle of the Fulton recovery system.

during a quick overflight of the operators on the ground or in the water.

To develop the system, Fulton used a weather balloon, nylon line, and 10- to 15-pound weights. He made numerous pickup attempts to develop a reliable procedure, and, as the system matured, he had his son take motion pictures of the operation. Fulton took the film to Admiral Luis de Florez, who was then

U.S. Navy S-2 Tracker aircraft were used by UDT personnel during experimentation with the Fulton recovery system in the late 1950s and into the early 1960s.

the director of technical research at the CIA. Believing that the program could best be handled by the military, de Florez put Fulton in touch with the Office of Naval Research, where he was granted a development contract from their Air Programs Division.

Over the next few years, Fulton refined the air and ground equipment for the pickup system. He conducted numerous flights over the desert at El Centro, California using a Navy P-2V Neptune for the pickups. He gradually increased the weight of the pickup until the line began to break. A braided nylon line with 4,000 pound test strength solved the problem. More vexing were the difficulties experienced with the locking

device, or sky anchor, that secured the line to the aircraft. Fulton eventually resolved this problem, which he considered the most demanding part of the entire developmental process.

By 1958, the Fulton Skyhook had taken its final shape. A kit that could easily be parachuted from an aircraft contained the necessary ground equipment for a pickup. It featured a harness for cargo

A UDT test subject being retrieved aboard a U.S. Navy S-2 Tracker during a daylight test in the early 1960s.

or personnel that was attached to a 500-foot, high-strength, braided nylon line. A portable helium bottle inflated a dirigible-shaped balloon, raising the line to its full height. The Skyhook-equipped aircraft would fly into the braded nylon line, aiming at a bright Mylar marker placed at the 425-foot level. As the line was snagged between the yoke of the aircraft, the balloon was released. Simultaneously, a spring-loaded trigger mechanism ("Sky Anchor") secured the line to the aircraft. As the line streamlined under the fuselage, it was snared by the pickup crew, using a J-hook, attached to a powered winch, and men or equipment were reeled on board. The aircraft also had cables strung from the nose to the wingtips to keep the balloon line away from the propellers, in case the catch was unsuccessful.

The first human pickup was on 12 August 1958, when Marine Corps Staff Sergeant Levi W. Woods was winched on board a P2V. During the same period, several UDT personnel, including the author, couldn't resist the challenge of experimenting with

Two test subjects wear the pick-up suits. Behind them is the package containing the balloon and helium tanks.

Sequence showing the complete process of retrieving UDT men from the ground. These photographs were taken at Turner Field, Naval Amphibious Base, Coronado, California in October 1965.

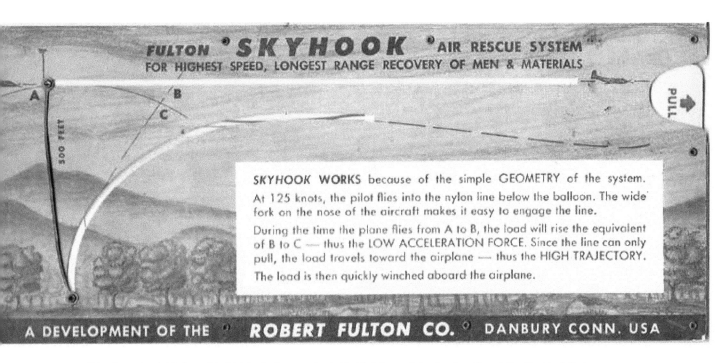

# FULTON "SKYHOOK" AIR RESCUE SYSTEM

## FOR HIGHEST SPEED, LONGEST RANGE RECOVERY OF MEN & MATERIALS

PULL →

**SKYHOOK WORKS** because of the simple GEOMETRY of the system.

At 125 knots, the pilot flies into the nylon line below the balloon. The wide fork on the nose of the aircraft makes it easy to engage the line.

During the time the plane flies from A to B, the load will rise the equivalent of B to C — thus the LOW ACCELERATION FORCE. Since the line can only pull, the load travels toward the airplane — thus the HIGH TRAJECTORY.

The load is then quickly winched aboard the airplane.

A DEVELOPMENT OF THE **ROBERT FULTON CO.** DANBURY CONN. USA

We all received this four sided folder before our tests that briefly explains the function of the Sky-Hook System.

**The Fulton SKYHOOK** is to pickup and rescue operations what the parachute is to delivery and bail-out operations. It is now possible with a fixed wing airplane in flight to recover personnel and equipment safely, reliably, easily and on a worldwide scale. Thousands of tests and operations have been conducted with cargo loads and personnel, single and dual, by land and sea, day and night, fair weather and foul, to provide a proven, effective system.

Spectacular as it is simple, SKYHOOK makes possible operations heretofore undreamed of. It is a new aerospace tool for rescue, for science and for industry.

**THE PICKUP** applies approximately 5 G's for one-half second, less than an average parachute jump.

**REELING IN** load takes 4 minutes. It's like riding in a rocking chair. No problems breathing or stabilizing.

**NIGHT RECOVERIES** are routine. Here a trained C-130 rescue crew brings its man aboard in the dark.

**WATER OR LAND PICK-UPS** are equally easy. Raft or ship-deck both provide good operating platforms.

**2-MAN PICKUPS** are performed either side by side or in tandem. It makes for a jolly ride.

# 3 STEPS
## TO RESCUE

SKYHOOK is so simple that within 10 to 15 minutes after the kit is parachute dropped (depending upon your familiarity with the equipment) you can be ready for pick up. The kit contains illustrated instructions. There are only three main steps to be taken . . .

**1** Open Bag 1 and put on harness-suit. At time of pickup it will adjust itself to your size, provide comfortable seat and be good windbreaker even in sub-zero weather.

**2** Remove balloon from Bag 2, plug in hose from helium bottle and inflate until arrows meet. When gas in one end of container is exhausted, switch to hose at other end.

**3** Open neck of Bag 3, release balloon, then sit down with back to wind. At night turn on lights with switch in right leg pocket. Airplane crew will do the rest.

# PROJECT COLDFEET: SEVEN DAYS IN THE ARCTIC

## FULTON SKYHOOK AND COLD WAR INTELLIGENCE

The first operational use of the Skyhook was under Project COLDFEET. The U.S. Intelligence Community pursued an opportunity to infiltrate an abandoned Soviet drift station on a floating ice deep in the Arctic.

During the Cold War, the United States and the Soviet Union battled for every advantage, including studying the Arctic for its strategic value. For seven days in May 1962, the US intelligence community pursued a rare opportunity to collect intelligence firsthand from an abandoned Soviet research station high in the Arctic.

The Soviet drift station, located on a floating ice island, had been hastily evacuated when shifting ice made the base aircraft runway unusable. Since the ice was breaking apart, and normal air transport to the island was now impossible, the Soviets felt the remote base and its equipment and research materials would be crushed and thoroughly destroyed in the Arctic Sea. Unfortunately for the Soviets, they were wrong.

A plan was quickly developed to parachute men on to the site, and to retrieve them using the Skyhook. Project COLDFEET was truly a joint venture bringing together the resources and expertise of the Office of Naval Research, the Defense Intelligence Agency, and the Central Intelligence Agency. On May 28, using pilots and a B-17 from CIA proprietary Intermountain Aviation—accompanied by a polar navigator borrowed from Pan American Airlines: Two intelligence collectors, Lieutenant Leonard LeSchack (who conceived the plan), and Air Force Major James Smith, were successfully dropped by parachute onto the ice.

The B-17, now rigged with Robert Fulton's Skyhook, returned on June 2 to recover the team and their take. The Skyhook was a unique airborne pickup device that included a nose yolk and a special winch system. The key measure of COLDFEET's success was the unprecedented safe removal of the investigative team and many critical items.

The mission yielded valuable information to the US intelligence community on the Soviet Union's drift station research activities. The team found evidence of advanced acoustical systems research to detect under-ice US submarines and efforts to develop Arctic anti-submarine warfare techniques.

This small team—incredibly courageous and resourceful—planned and executed a remarkable feat, capitalizing on a rare intelligence opportunity.

the Fulton recovery system. Testing was accomplished using the U.S. Navy's S-2 Tracker and RC-45J photo reconnaissance aircraft. Test and training events were accomplished on the West Coast at Coronado, California by UDT-11 and UDT-12 and on the East Coast at Norfolk, Virginia by UDT-21 and, later, UDT-22 and SEAL operators. As commanding officer of UDT-11, I had the opportunity to be an experimental test subject for Skyhook testing.

Because of the geometry involved, the person being picked up experienced less of a shock than during a parachute opening. After initial contact with the aircraft, the men describe the sensation as akin to a "swift kick in the pants." Once the line was captured, the operators being retrieved rose vertically at a slow rate to about 100 feet, then began to streamline behind the aircraft. Each operator controlled his stability by using arms and legs to prevent oscillation while being winched aboard.

On 26 June 1964, Photographer's Mate Jim Fox, a Petty Officer Third Class of UDT-22, was killed during a Skyhook training event. Two events were planned for that day. The first was a morning pick up from the Naval Amphibious Base beach to simulate a jungle rescue, which went off without a hitch. The second was a pick up from an inflatable raft in the afternoon. Fox was the afternoon test subject. He was successfully snatched by a Navy RC-45J aircraft, however, while being reeled in, a segment of the tow line snapped; dropping him away from the plane. As described by the author Orr Kelly: "Suddenly there was a loud pop, the line parted, and Fox fell away toward the surface of the bay, some 700 feet below." Fox had no parachute, since the Fulton system didn't employ them, and, sadly, he fell to his death in the Chesapeake Bay. Also, according to Mr. Kelly, "Fulton was deeply concerned, hurried down to examine the Skyhook to determine what had gone wrong. He found that the winch had not been turned off as Fox came into the plane, but had continued to turn until it snapped the nylon line." Jim Fox's hometown newspaper in Maryland, the *Cumberland Evening Times*, reported his death.

**BURIAL AT SEA** — Navy frogman James E. Fox, formerly of Cumberland, who fell 600 feet to his death in Chesapeake Bay from a helicopter when a ladder collapsed, will be buried at sea at his wife's request. The seven-year Navy veteran met his death near Virginia Beach, Va.

Despite the accident and death of Jim Fox, the UDT and SEAL men were not deterred, and continued training with the Fulton system. The last training event was a nighttime pickup off the beaches of Coronado, California on 20 October 1965. A pair of two-man teams swam out from the beach, where inflatable boats with Fulton equipment were air

# CAPTAIN NORMAN OLSON'S EXPERIENCE

## FULTON SKYHOOK TEST SUBJECT

We didn't know what to expect. Chief Pete Slempa and I bobbed around in the pitch black of the ocean off San Diego waiting for the plane to drop the Skyhook bundle. Unfortunately, it was dropped far from us, so we had to swim for it. We were exhausted when we got there. We inflated the rubber boat, climbed aboard, then struggled to get the overalls on—not easy to do in a rubber boat at night while being tossed in the Pacific Ocean.

Then we inflated the dirigible that takes the nylon line up into the air. The thing was huge—the size of a room of a house—and took three bottles of helium to inflate. As the balloon began to inflate, the wind caught it, and we struggled to get it into the air. In the process it hooked on some equipment, and then Pop! The thing collapsed.

Dr. Fulton was on a safety boat, and was fit to be tied. He motored over to us and said: "We have never had any problems like this before. The Army Special Forces have done this dozens of times without problems."

We were in luck because they had an extra dirigible on the safety boat, so with their help, we had another go at it and successfully inflated the balloon and lofted the line.

Because it was night, I wore a battery pack for the strobes, which allowed the plane to see us in the ocean and the balloon above us. I turned on the strobe, and then zap! There was a short and sparks started flying and burning me. I got the thing off fast.

Again, the safety boat came over with Dr. Fulton. He asked us, "What happened?"

I said, "I don't know. You tell me."

We pulled in the dirigible, an exhausting process, so that Dr. Fulton could tinker with the electronics and fix it. Then up it went again.

I told Chief Slempa: "Let me tell you something. If this shorts again, we are going to live with it. I'm not wrestling that dirigible again. As soon as the plane hits the line, the sparking will be over because the circuit will be broken."

When I turned on the strobe, the same thing happened. Gritting the electrical shocks, I yelled, "Okay Pete, hang on there. We are going to be taken."

The plane came in and snagged us. We were jerked vertically up about 500 feet from a standstill, hanging on by that line with so much pressure on it that it stretched as thin as a thread. That made me very nervous. But soon you get used to it. The view was beautiful. We were streaming along the coast from San Diego to La Jolla with a gorgeous view of the skyline.

Then all of the sudden there was a sharp drop, and I thought we were done for. My first thought was that I wished I had a parachute. It turned out they were adjusting the winch mechanism, which caused a few problems and more than one stomach-turning drop. It took a full 20 minutes to bring us into the plane. The pilot made lazy circles up and down the coast so that we could at least enjoy the view.

Finally, they winched us up close enough so that we could see the bottom of the plane. The noise was tremendous and the wind buffeted us. We were just about in there, when the winch chugged again and dropped us. Again, I thought we were finished, but thankfully, we were still attached. They started hauling us in. In all, it was a four-hour ordeal.

dropped to them. After donning the coveralls with built-in harnesses, the first team sent its balloon up and was successfully recovered; as was the second boat team. The second team included Lieutenant Maynard Weyers in the top position and Boatswain's Mate Second Class Jerome Cozart below him. According to Lieutenant Weyers, because the weight of the men and the low power of the support aircraft, it took 21 minutes to retrieve the pair.

Shortly after this training event, UDT and SEAL leaders decided that there was little to be gained by having the men practice being whisked into the air, which took no skill and detracted from more significant training needs.

Although discontinued by the UDT and SEAL Teams, the Fulton air recovery system was used by others from 1965 to 1996 on several variants of the C-130 Hercules including the MC-130s and HC-130s. The capability was eventually transferred to the U.S. Air Force Special Operations Command (AFSOC). With the increased availability of long-range helicopters such as AFSOCs MH-53 Pave Low, HH-60 Pave Hawk, the U.S. Army Special Operations Command MH-47 Chinook, and now the CV-22 tilt-rotor aircraft—all with in-flight refueling capability, the Fulton "Skyhook" system became old technology. Thus, in September 1996, AFSOC ceased maintaining the capability.

## Fulton Maritime Recovery System

Before the air recovery system, Robert Fulton developed a recovery system for UDT men clustered in the water. This development occurred after Fulton visited UDT Commander Doug "Red Dog" Fane at his

Fulton Maritime Recovery System being used with a MK IV LCPL by UDT men at their training base at St. Thomas, USVI. Note the rigging on the bow, two sleds, and men being recovered by a ramp attached to the stern. The LCPL didn't have enough power to pick up more that a few men simultaneously.

headquarters at the Naval Amphibious Base in Coronado, California. The two men discussed ways to improve recovering swimmers from the water after operations—particularly when under enemy fire.

The method for recovering swimmers by high-speed small craft was first developed by the UDT men in the Pacific during World War II, and had changed over time only to accommodate different varieties of boats. Before each mission, the men would be transported to the beach in their support craft containing an inflatable boat. To begin the mission, the inflatable boat would be secured to the side of the support craft. While at the objective, the boat was guided in a straight line parallel to the beach. When directed, the men would individually climb out of the support craft and into the inflatable boat, where they would be placed into the water at 25-yard intervals -- the separation they need to accomplish their reconnaissance.

After reconnoitering enemy-held beaches, the men would swim several hundred yards back out to sea and line up in a straight line--again at 25-yard intervals. Their recovery craft, towing the inflatable boat, would then line up on the men with the inflatable boat toward the sea side to aid in protecting the men for enemy fire. As the recovery craft approached, the man being recovered would raise his left arm straight up and kick very hard to obtain as much elevation out of the water as possible. A UDT operator in the inflatable boat would act as the "snare man," and, as his title would indicate, used a rubber-hose-like device to hook the swimmer's arm and snare him out of the water and into the inflatable. From there, the UDT operator would climb into the support craft. This method stood the test of time and was very reliable, however, it was also somewhat slow and permitted recovery of only one swimmer at a time; leaving the others in the water exposed to potential enemy fire. Moreover, if one swimmer in the pick-up line was missed, the boat would have to circle around and snare him again.

UDT operators casting from the swimmer compartment at the stern of the LCSR. The men jump to attain intervals of approximately 25 yards.

Fulton immediately realized that the Skyhook concept might be adaptable to small craft, and, in so doing, could provide for mass-swimmer recovery. The system was developed and first attempted with the

UDT operators being towed back aboard the LCSR in the Fulton sled.

ort and starboard views of the LCSR carrying the stacked sleds used for the Fulton maritime recovery system. The winch can clearly be seen on the ow of the boat.

Mark IV Landing Craft, Personnel, Large (LCPLs), boats that were common within the UDT inventory, and the ame craft taken on deployments with the Amphibious Force. This is the same boat that was used for the hook nd snare method, which had a design speed of 19 knots at full load. A full load for UDT men involved more han the men themselves, since often they would require several tons of demolitions and other equipment. It s rare that the LCPL actually achieved its design speed in any kind of sea state. In any case, tests determined hat it was very under-powered in performing the Fulton recovery method reliably.

The capability became much more accomplishable with the introduction of the Landing Craft, Swimmer Reconnaissance (LCSR) craft into the Naval Special Warfare Boat Support Unit (BSU) inventory. The LCSR had a speed of 40+ knots and was powered by a gas-turbine engine, thus, it now had the power and speed needed.

The Fulton Maritime System was comprised of two small sleds that were six-feet long and manufactured with buoyant foam. Several hundred feet of polypropylene line connected the sleds, and was launched with he sled. This line had a guide-on buoy placed in the middle, which provided an aim point for the boat's coxswain. A long rod was attached to the bow just below the waterline to capture the line for a winch on the bow of the boat. A ramp was secured to the back of the boat to capture the sleds once they were winched to the back of the boat.

The LCSR was a large combatant craft with a swimmer's cabin in the after area of the boat. To cast into he water, UDT men would simply jump off of the stern and into the boat's wake at approximately 25-yard ntervals. Their subsequent recovery employed the Fulton System. To accomplish a pick-up or recovery, the UDT men would cluster together in two groups as the LCSR made a high-speed pass by them and drop off he sleds several hundred feet apart. The LCSR then proceeded in a large arc and came back around to pick-up the UDT men in the water by aiming at the float in the middle of the polypropylene line. The LCSR would

This photograph of the LCSR provides a look at the winch located behind the anchor on the bow, and the two recovery sleds mounted on top of the swimmer cabin.

steer until the bow rod snagged the float line and guided it up from the water and into the winch located on the bow. After snag was accomplished, the LCSR proceeded away from the beach as the sled and men were winched-in. The recovery was completed when both sleds were brought to the recovery ramp and the men climbed on to the boat.

The Fulton Maritime Recovery System lived a very short life in the UDT and SEAL Teams. The LCSR, with adequate speed and power, could easily accomplish the cast and recovery; however, the boat had many technical difficulties, the gas-turbine engines were very noisy, and the engines were maintenance intensive. Moreover, the LCSR could not be launched and recovered aboard ship; making the capability nearly impossible to deploy overseas. A decision was made to eliminate the boat from the active inventory, and the Fulton System went with it.

# CHAPTER 12

# SEAL AIR DELIVERY CAPABILITIES

It was mentioned in Chapter 1 that capabilities were attempted with helicopters in the late 1940s and early 1950s by the Underwater Demolition Teams, which were the forerunners of today's SEAL Teams. This was the period leading up to the Korean War.

There is no evidence that the UDTs used helicopters tactically during the Korean War period, but air capabilities experimentation resumed after Korea. Substantial operational capabilities were attempted and many were adopted. The men pioneered the helicopter "casting" technique by installing a "swing bar" at the door of the aircraft to assist water entry. The swing bar was adopted after operators first tried simply jumping out of the helicopter, which often resulted in bad body position upon impact with the water. Someone came up with the idea to mount a bar on the outside of the helicopter. The men would accomplish water entry by

UDT operators experimenting with cast and recovery from a Sikorsky H-34 helicopter flown by U.S. Navy and U.S. Marine Corps pilots circa 1955-1960..

These rare color photographs from the mid 1950s show UDT operators dropping from a swing bar, then using a caving ladder to climb back into the Sikorsky H-34 helicopter.

sitting in the door of the helicopter with their legs outside, and, when directed, would simply grasp the bar and swing into the air and release—all the while maintaining a rigid body position for water entry.

To accomplish water insertion safely, it was discovered, after many uncontrolled and painful water-smacking impacts, that, if the helicopter maintained a corresponding altitude and speed, for example 20 knots speed at an altitude of 20 feet, the water landing could be accomplished without undue pain or injury. This, of course, had much to do with the skill of the pilots, and their ability to maintain the desired altitude and speed. If the helicopter drifted upward, it could be a long fall for the UDT men. For recovery, the men climbed up and into the helicopter using caving ladders. Helicopter cast and recovery operational techniques were refined as aircraft designs improved, and remains in practical use today in different forms.

## SEALs and Seawolves in Vietnam

Serious tactical operations with helicopters didn't really occur until the SEAL Teams were formed in January 1962. Moreover, they were not commonly employed until after February 1966, when SEAL direct-action platoons were deployed to Vietnam. As SEAL operations in Vietnam expanded, their need for helicopter support grew exponentially.

It was during Vietnam that the SEALs found their now-storied operating elements (sea in the form of dirty, tidal water, air from helicopters and land in the jungles) in the delta regions of South Vietnam. While tactical mobility was largely accomplished by boats, helicopters were often used to accomplish aerial reconnaissance before a mission, for insertion and extraction of personnel during quick-strike raids, and they were also used extensively for gunship support. This support came initially with U.S. Army helicopters and later by the U.S. Navy Seawolf helicopters deployed in support of Commander, Task Force 116 (CTF-116) for mission tasking surrounding Operation GAME WARDEN.

## BILL BRUHMULLER REMEMBERS

### EARLY HELICOPTER EXPERIMENTS

Navy SEAL Bill Bruhmuller, who retired as a Master Chief, was in on the early helicopter cast and recovery training and development. He provided this first-hand account:

I was very fortunate in the early days to be selected for many test groups. I worked on early helicopter cast and recovery methods. One of our projects was to learn how to use helicopters for quick insertion onto beach areas.

We were down at Camp Lejeune in North Carolina for a week. Each day, we would chopper out about 50 feet from the beach. We had to experiment to find a good speed for exit (called casting). Then we had to figure out the best body position. It was a painful process of learning — as in "Wow! I'm not going to do that again."

We used ladders for recovery. They would dangle a caving ladder out the door of the helo and we would grab onto a rung and climb up. That was painless. Getting out of the helicopter was a different thing. We developed the idea to position a bar out the door so you could hang out there and position your body, which is hard to do if you simply jump. You are only up at 20 or 35 feet, so you don't have time. We would jump at a moderate forward pace, not just in a hover. You hung on the bar and positioned for the perfect technique. Dropping gear from helicopters came much later in the 1960s.

A Seawolf UH-1 "Huey" helicopter from the Helicopter Attack Light Squadron THREE.

SEALs in Vietnam operated in small elements that could include as few as four men and, rarely, in a platoon of 14 men. SEAL platoons operated for the most part in the Delta Region of South Vietnam, where they penetrated Viet Cong and North Vietnamese Army refuges to collect intelligence and destroy or capture VC infrastructures, which included: Personnel, equipment, guns, ammunition, and housing strongholds. SEALs operated primarily (and preferably) at night; using the cover of darkness and silent tactics and techniques to reach target objectives. Often, however, they would meet unexpected resistance, and required assistance in the form of gunfire support.

HAL-3's Squadron logo.

A HAL-3 Seawolf helicopter underway in Vietnam.

U.S. Navy helicopter support was established for CTF-116 in 1966; initially by detachments from the Navy's Helicopter Combat Support Squadron (HCS-1) deployed from the United States, known as "Fleet Angels," and later by Helicopter Attack Light Squadron (HAL-3), known as "Seawolfs," whose support was much more reliable. HAL-3 was actually established in Vietnam in April 1967 as a dedicated in-country asset to CTF 116, thus, replacing HCS-1, which was based in Imperial Beach, California.

SEAL platoon and Seawolf detachments were often co-located at various locations throughout the Delta and, thus, became closely bonded. Seawolf crews were briefed about the place and duration before each SEAL mission, and were standing ready and "on call" in the event SEALs needed assistance. Moreover, Seawolf crews often accomplished missions considered "outside the operating envelope" of the UH-1 "Huey" helicopters they flew. Configured as gunships, Seawolf helicopters were armed with 2.75-inch rocket launchers and M-60 machine guns on each side. Rapid fire mini-guns were later added.

They often would provde provide gunship support on operations. The SEALs could count on the Seawolfs to engage the VC at night; often when SEALs were in very close contact with the enemy. The SEALs could always rest assured that Seawolf support would remain with them until they could be safely extracted by boat or by other helicopters. Seawolf crews supported SEALs exceptionally in extremis situations; often performing Medical Evacuation functions or exfiltrating SEALs, often dumping weapons and ammunition, if necessary, to lighten the helicopter to accommodate the additional weight of the SEALs and their equipment.

## Helicopter Support Post-Vietnam

HAL-3 was the first U.S. Navy Helicopter Attack Squadron ever established, and it was the only such squadron established and disestablished outside of the United States. Unlike the SEALs, the capability provided by HAL-3 did not survive after the Vietnam War. The squadron was disestablished on 16 March 1972 in Vietnam. There were many attempts by the Naval Special Warfare community to revive this somewhat dedicated capability. As a result, in July 1976, Helicopter Attack Squadron (Light) Four (HAL-4), a Naval Reserve Component, was established in Norfolk, Virginia. The squadron provided non-deployed insertion/extraction and direct fire support training for SEALs and other Navy units.

HAL-4 continued supporting U.S.-based training operations, and in October 1989 was re-designated Helicopter Combat Support Special Squadron 4 (HSC-4). Along with a change in designation, HSC-4 received the new HH-60H Seahawk helicopter and added Combat Search and Rescue (CSAR) to its primary mission of Naval Special Warfare support. In

Logo of HSC-84, the Red Wolves.

December 1990, the squadron was mobilized and sent to Saudi Arabia to support Operations DESERT STORM and DESERT SHIELD, where, for the first time since Vietnam, a U.S. Navy helicopter squadron provided direct support to SEALs and other Special Operations Forces. HSC-4 deployed in September 1994 to support SEALs in Operation UPHOLD DEMOCRACY in Haiti, and deployed to the Central Command in support of Operation IRAQI FREEDOM. During October 2006, HSC-4 was re-designated Helicopter Sea Combat Squadron 84 (HSC-84); called the "Red Wolves," and since 2008, with HSC-85, supported the CENTCOM Joint Special Operations Air Component to support SEALs and coalition special operations missions. HSC-85, known as the "Firehawks," headquartered at the Naval Air Station North Island, San Diego, was transitioned from being a logistical support squadron to its new mission of NSW support in July 2001.

A U.S. Navy HH-60H Seahawk helicopter used by the "Red Wolves" of Helicopter Sea Combat Squadron FOUR (HSC-4) to support U.S. Navy SEALs and other Special Operations Forces.

A HH-60H Sea Hawk helicopter flown by HSC-85 approaches a gas and oil platform during a training operation with Navy SEALs.

An HH-60H from HSC-84 recovering an operator via a caving ladder during pre-deployment training in 2014.

Logo of HSC-85, the Firehawks.

In Balad, Iraq on 25 August 2008, HSC-84, conducted night operation in the Central Command area of operation. HSC-84 was the only Navy component of the Combined Joint Special Operations Air Component (CJSOAC), and was supporting vital special operations missions in the Iraqi theatre.

As a result of the deployment of HSC-84 in Operation IRAQI FREEDOM, Admiral (SEAL) Eric Olson, then commander of the U.S. Special Operations Command, requested that HSC-84 and HSC-85 be shifted to full-time special operations support. As a result of this request, both squadrons deployed detachments to the Central Command area of operation to support SEALs and other Special Operations Forces. HSC squadrons usually deployed detachments of two helicopters with maintenance crews and support staff.

Sadly, in March 2016, the Red Wolves were disestablished owing to budget cuts imposed by the Congressional Sequester. Plans were being made to restructure HSC-85 as something the Navy calls Tactical Support Units (TSUs), with a similar TSU on the East Coast. Part of the plan was to switch to the MH-60 "Knighthawk" helicopter.

# CHAPTER 13

# NSW AIR DELIVERY CAPABILITIES

Helicopters and most recently tilt-rotor aircraft have been considered for a host of operational support capabilities involving Naval Special Warfare SEAL and Special Boat Teams. When helicopters with better lift capacity became available in the 1960s, UDT and SEAL frogmen began experimenting with them to deliver equipment as well as men. With the exception of parachuting, operations, actions, and activities with fixed-winged aircraft didn't evolve until the late 1970s. Over the years, innovative of methods for air delivery of boats, SDVs and other vehicles have been devised, tested, and perfected or rejected.

## SEAL Team Assault Boat (STAB)

Probably the first attempt to move boats by air involved the SEAL Team Assault Boat (STAB) being developed by SEAL Team TWO in the mid-1960s. The STAB capability was the brainchild of Lieutenant Jack Macione at SEAL Team TWO. Up until that time, SEALs had no dedicated boats in their inventory, thus, operations in Vietnam forced them to rely on others. Gus Kosar, who was always rigging different things to throw out the back of airplanes and off the sides of helicopters, got together with Jack to rig up something new. Based on Lieutenant Macione's design, and a bit of trial and error, the STAB evolved. It was a modified Boston Whaler with an overall length of 21 feet and a draft of 31 inches with a full load. Armament included seven hull pintle positions, which would accept 50 cal. machine guns, MK 18 Honeywell Grenade Launchers, or M-60 machine

During experimental testing, a Navy CH-46 helicopter is seen transporting a SEAL Team Assault Boat (STAB) developed by SEAL Team TWO. The STAB was later deployed to Vietnam, but none were used operationally after being transported by air.

STAB seen at the SEAL Team TWO compound at Little Creek, Virginia.

guns. Operational experience, however, proved that only the swing mounts and center mounts were suitable for the 50 cal. machine guns. One-quarter inch armor plating was placed along each side of the cockpit area and on each side of the coxswain's seat. The boat was designed specifically for use in Vietnam.

During its development, several attempts were made to transport the STAB by helicopter, which resulted in some painful lessons. In what became a recurring theme, testing often resulted in unintended drops with unfortunate results. When Lieutenant Macione attempted to transport one of his STAB prototypes to the ocean, the helicopter crew chief lost control of the boat and let it go. It crashed to smithereens. Lieutenant Macione looked like he had lost a child. Thankfully we had made two of them. There is an old frogman saying: "Two is one and one is none." That proved true in this case.

# Light SEAL Support Craft (LSSC)

The LSSC (Light SEAL Support Craft) was designed for squad-sized operations in Vietnam. It was an aluminum 24-foot long boat with a low silhouette and a nine-foot beam. The boat came with radar and numerous gun positions, including a .50 caliber

SEALs under way in a STAB on the rivers of South Vietnam.

Water-level view of a Light SEAL Support Craft (LSSC) ready to get underway with a squad of SEALs.

machine gun on the stern. The cockpit, crew, and engine compartments were protected with ceramic armor plating. The LSSC was a workhorse for the SEALs in the Delta Region of South Vietnam. No known air-delivered operations were conducted.

## Swimmer (Later SEAL) Delivery Vehicle

Once the Mark 7 Swimmer Delivery Vehicle (MK 7 SDV) had been introduced into fleet service during the late 1960s, there immediately became an urgency to improve its tactical mobility. No reliable submarine capability had yet emerged; although the USS Tunney

A Light SEAL Support Craft (LSSC) being transported by a U.S. Army CH-47 Chinook helicopter. No information accompanied this photograph. It appears to be an experimental test or an administrative lift of the LSSC. The LSSC was never transported tactically.

in the Pacific had been converted for UDT combat swimmer use. It was a former Regulus missile-carrying submarine, and its missile chamber had been converted for diver use; eventually to include SDV launch and recovery. SDVs transported by amphibious surface ships were often difficult to launch and recover; especially in any kind of seas and with poor ship handling systems. It didn't take long for the men to try something with helicopters, where things didn't always go as planned.

A U.S. Navy MH-53E Sea Dragon Airborne Mine Countermeasures helicopter tests its capability to transport a MK 8 SEAL Delivery Vehicle during experimentation at the Naval Coastal Systems Center, Panama City, Florida.

Master Chief Bill Bruhmuller recalled: "There is one incident that stands out. We were on base at Little Creek, Virginia Beach, Virginia. We went to a field, where a Navy CH-46 picked up an SDV to fly it out over the beach. We were probably a half mile from the water near the golf course. The helicopter with the SDV slung underneath headed for the Chesapeake Bay, and for reasons unknown, the helicopter's pickup cable snapped, and the SDV fell on a guy's car in the parking lot. It must have been fun for him to have to call the police to tell them a miniature submarine had landed on his car, and that he had no idea how it got there. By then, I assure you, we were long gone."

Another incident occurred when the UDTs at Little Creek were assisting the Marine Corps with their interest in acquiring an SDV capability. The Marines had acquired three MK 7 SDVs, and the UDT men were providing operator and maintenance training. The Marines, also seeking expanded tactical mobility options, attempted to lift and deliver an SDV by helicopter. This event took place at the Little Creek Naval Amphibious Base. Once the USMC helicopter took off with the SDV underneath, the SDV began to swing out of control, and to prevent endangering the helicopter and crew, they cut away the SDV, which ended its future operational career. It smashed to pieces near the Amphibious Base golf course. The Marines quickly determined that the SDV capability was not for them and ended further testing.

Later attempts were accomplished in a Navy laboratory setting as the newer MK 8 SDV was entering fleet service. The NSW-SDV development and support program had been centralized at the Naval Coastal Systems Center, Panama City, FL. The requirement for expanded SDV tactical transport was always looming, and Panama City took on the task. Transporting SDVs tactically by helicopter proved to be a difficult challenge.

Remains of a MK 7 SDV after being accidently dropped on the Naval Amphibious Base, Little Creek golf course.

MK 7 SDV, like the one dropped in a parking lot, is seen underway.

## Maritime Craft Aerial Deployment System

The 11-meter Naval Special Warfare Rigid Inflatable Boat (RIB).

The Naval Special Warfare 11-meter Rigid Inflatable Boat (RIB) is employed by Naval Special Warfare's Special Warfare Combatant-craft Crewmen (SWCC) within the Special Boat Teams (SBTs). It is a high-speed, high-buoyancy, and extreme weather craft assigned the primary mission of insertion and extraction of SEAL tactical elements conducting Over the Beach (OTB) or shipboard seize and search operations among others.

MCADS being loaded aboard a U.S. Air Force C-130 aircraft.

MCADS being extracted from the ramp of a U.S. Air Force C-17 over the Pacific Ocean near Guam.

After being pulled out of a MC-130 aircraft with a drag parachute, the MCADS platform can be seen separating from the 11-meter NSW Rigid Inflatable Boat before its parachutes are deployed.

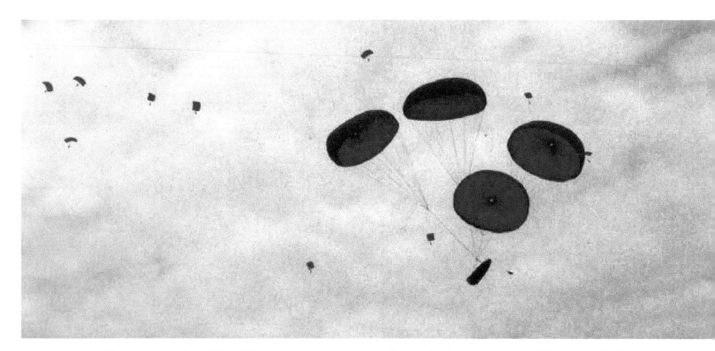

The NSW 11-meter Rigid Inflatable Boat (RIB) under canopy; followed by jumpers that include SWCCs and SEALs.

The NSW RIB has, for many years, served as NSW's workhorse combatant craft with air-delivery attributes that substantially enhanced its capability for worldwide, no-notice deployments.

These missions are made possible by employment of SBT-20's Maritime Craft Aerial Deployment System (MCADS). MCADS involves rigging each 11-meter RIB with four large parachutes and dropping the fully laden combat-equipped boat from the back of USAF C-130 or C-17 aircraft at an altitude of 3,500-feet. An extractor parachute pulls the load from the aircraft.

The boat and platform separate immediately after leaving the aircraft, and both descend to the water under their own parachutes. The MCADS platform lands separately, and operationally it will be configured to sink immediately. During training evolutions, however, the MCADS is rigged with flotation for recovery and re-use. The MCADS mission involves delivery of SEALs or other Special Operations Forces operators to any potential target of interest, or to conduct SWCC specific missions.

Once the MCADS and RIB are launched from the support aircraft, four SWCC operators immediately parachute out with the boat and follow it into the water. Within 20 minutes SWCCs have the boat unpacked and rigged to get underway. The 11-meter NSW RIB is currently being replaced with a family of advanced technology boats called Combat Craft Medium (CCM) and Combatant Craft Assault (CCA).

A NSW 11-meter Rigid Inflatable Boat delivered by MCADS ready to gently hit the water.

A Special Warfare Combatant-Craft Crewmen (SWCC) follows the 11-meter RIB into the water.

## Maritime External Air Transportation System

The Special Operation Craft-Riverine (SOC-R) is operated and maintained by Special Boat Team 22 (SBT-22), which is headquartered at the Spaceflight Center in Stennis, Mississippi. SWCC operators perform short-range insertion and extraction of SEALs and other Special Operations Forces in riverine, inland waterways, and near-shore environments.

The SOC-R carries a crew of four that include a helmsman and three gunners, and has the capacity to carry eight combat-equipped SEALs and their mission-support equipment. The SOC-R was designed to be operationally transported by, but not parachuted from, U.S. Air Force C-130 or larger military aircraft. For tactical transport from a forward operating base or ship, SBT-12, SBT-20 and SBT-22 have developed a tactical insertion and extraction air delivery capability using the Maritime Extraction Air-Transportation

A Marine Corps CH-53 helicopter lifts an 11-meter NSW Rigid Inflatable Boat (RIB) from Special Boat Team 12 (SBT-12, using the Maritime External Air Transportation System (MEATS).

System (MEATS). MEATS allows an Army CH-47D or Navy or Marine Corps CH-53 helicopter to carry a SOC-R, or 11-meter NSW RIB, rigged to the underbelly of the helicopter with slings. SWCC operators use a fast ropping technique to descend from the helicopter onto the SOC-R or NSW RIB for insertions, and a ladder dropped down for recovery into helicopter for extraction and return to the forward operating base.

SWCC operators rig their RIB to a CH-47D while underway. The men will secure the boat for transport then climb into the helicopter.

Special Operations Craft, Riverine (SOC-R) under a U.S. Army Special Operations Command CH-47 for recovery and transport back to base.

# CHAPTER 14

# SEAL TACTICAL INSERTION CAPABILITIES

SEALs have adopted and adapted a variety of techniques for arriving at various objectives through the air. This chapter outlines some of the primary capabilities.

## Fast Roping

Fast roping is a tactic and technique acquired from the British military. It is formally known as the Fast Rope Insertion and Extraction System (FRIES); although that acronym is rarely ever used by U.S. Navy SEALs. Moreover, the technique cannot be used for extraction, so the name is misleading. Fast roping is a technique used to insert an assault force from support aircraft in a matter of seconds.

During late 1970s, I was overall commander of the UDT and SEAL Teams in the Atlantic Fleet. During this period, SEALs were tasked with a training exercise involving the capture of an offshore oil platform that had been taken over by terrorists, and this was a relatively new task for them. The exercise was planned and conducted using rappelling and other techniques, but these were lacking and pointed out deficiencies in our training and capabilities.

The British Special Air Service (SAS), SEAL counterparts in the United Kingdom, had developed

Navy SEALs practice fast roping on to the deck of an U.S. Navy Amphibious ship during training with a U.S. Navy HH-60H helicopter.

the fast roping capability. The British were ahead of others on this capability, largely because they had been dealing with domestic terrorism from the Irish Republican Army for years.

As a result, 15 combat-experienced SEAL veterans were selected to go to England to learn the tactics, techniques, and procedures of fast roping and to assess and list the equipment required. Their trip was successful, and upon return, the men went to the Gulf of Mexico to train on oil rigs and other installations. Since then, fast roping emerged as one of the foremost capabilities needed in maritime and other special operations.

Fast roping is simple and indeed fast. A tactical rope can be rolled into a deployment bag with one end secured to the support aircraft with a safety pin. The original rope employed by the British was made out of smooth, thick nylon that could be used very much like a flexible fire pole. The ropes used today are employed in the same fashion, but have been improved. They are now braided with eight strands of nylon line in a pattern on the outer circumference that isn't smooth. This makes the rope easier to grip. The rope is olive-drab and approximately two inches in diameter to provide ease of handling and a sure grip with minimum stretch. Tactical ropes come in 50- to 120-foot lengths, which allow SEALs to insert onto various structures and

A squad of U.S. Navy SEALs training in GOPLAT (Gas and Oil Platform) boarding techniques. SEALs may be called upon to retake GOPLAT facilities from hostile hands in locations around the world.

U.S. Navy SEALs conduct an at-sea rendezvous by fast roping aboard a U.S. submarine.

Navy SEALs practicing a fast roping assault from a U.S. Navy "Red Wolves" helicopter against a U.S. Navy Amphibious Ship. Notice as one SEAL hits the deck; another is already descending on the rope.

U.S. Navy SEALs fast roping from a MH-6 "Little Bird" flown by the U.S. Army's 160th Special Operations Aviation Regiment (Airborne).

environments without the need for support aircraft to land.

Depending on the model of the helicopter or tilt-rotor aircraft, the rope might be installed outside on a hoist mechanism next to the side door or attached to a bracket off the back of the tail ramp and secured with the safety pin. Once over the insertion point, the rope is deployed and, even before it hits the ground, the SEALs are already jumping onto the rope and sliding down. It is extremely useful in rapid deployment situations, because an entire assault team can be inserted with 10 to 15 seconds. Unlike rappelling, once the SEAL operator hits the ground, he is free of the rope and can begin his mission. As soon as the SEALs are safely on the ground, one of the air crewman pulls the safety pin; allowing the rope to drop to the ground so as not to hinder further aircraft maneuvers.

Fast roping is most often used by SEALs in shipboard take-down situations. These are called Visit, Board, Seize, and Search (VBSS) operations, where an armed SEAL strike force must accomplish Maritime Interception Operations (MIO) by quickly boarding an underway passenger ship, commercial ship, or military ship under hostile or unknown tactical situations. Fast roping also allows SEALs to

In addition to U.S. Army and Navy helicopters, U.S. Air Force Special Operations Command CV-22 tilt-rotor aircraft provide a long-range insertion and extraction capability for U.S. Navy SEALs and other Special Operations Forces. Here, U.S. Navy SEALs are seen fast roping from hovering aircraft.

U.S. Navy SEALs fast rope onto a ship's deck from a U.S. Army MH-47 Chinook.

Navy SEALs fast rope aboard a MK V Special Operations Craft. They are training to perform an at-sea rendezvous with Special Warfare Combatant-craft Crewmen (SWCC) for a follow-on mission.

respond to crises as a quick-reaction force ashore, against gas and oil platforms, and to assault buildings as they did in the raid on the Osama Bin Laden compound.

## Rappelling

U.S. Navy SEALs have been rappelling since the early days of their inception in 1962. SEALs train in this tactic and technique to provide a capability to descend from a helicopter or the side of a building, ship, or steep terrain in mountain warfare situations. Rappelling allows the combat-equipped SEAL to manage his rate of descent, and, if and when necessary, have a free hand for firing a weapon or tossing a flash-bang or hand grenade to facilitate entry under hostile or unknown situations.

SEALs practice two kinds of rappelling. Foremost is mountain rappelling outlined above, where a rope is anchored to a cliff with artificial anchors like cams, pitons, bolts, or to natural anchors like trees and boulders. Usually the rope is either doubled with the midpoint at the anchors or tied to another climbing rope. The SEALs

In a fighting position on the side of a sheer cliff. (Photo courtesy of Rich Graham of Trident Fitness Tactical http://www.tridentfitness.net)

Former Navy SEAL Rich Graham preforms an Aussie style rappel off a 40+ foot bridge. (Photo courtesy of Rich Graham of Trident Fitness Tactical)

Navy SEALs practice rappelling from a U.S. Navy HH-60H helicopter.

132

then use a belay device and the friction of the rope to control descent as they literally slide down the fixed rope to the surface of land, building, or water. SEALs have taken rappelling to new levels by mastering the technique for descending from helicopters, tilt-rotor aircraft, buildings, and the sides of ships among others.

The second rappelling method is called the Australian rappel, which involves descending on a fixed rope in a face-down standing position. SEALs use this abseiling method for quickly assaulting a target while being able to see it and shoot at it if necessary. The Australian rappel is the simplest form of abseiling. Like mountain rappelling, speed is controlled by using a belay device attached to a harness round a SEAL's waist. SEALs hold the rope with one hand above and one hand below the device to control their speed. The belay device causes friction in the rope, making sure that they don't drop too fast. The technique derives from the Australian military and was first accomplished in the late 1960s, where it was called the "Carabiner Rundown." It has become known internationally as the Australian Rappel.

## McGuire Rig

An extremely crude device, the McGuire rig was used to extract soldiers from the jungles of Vietnam. It would be suspended from a helicopter and used in areas without a suitable pick-up zone. It was simple, inexpensive, and effective. Moreover, the harness didn't require the soldier to carry any special equipment. It was designed by Sergeant Major Charles T. McGuire, a member of Project DELTA, a U.S. Army Special Forces reconnaissance project in Vietnam. The system was capable of extracting up to six operators at a time in areas in the Vietnam jungle that were otherwise inaccessible.

The McGuire rig had two-inch wide webbing "saddle" slings attached to the end of a 150-200 foot-long rope, which was lowered from a hovering helicopter. Three ropes with McGuire Rigs attached could be dropped from a UH-1 "Huey" helicopter—all on the same side. A deployment pack containing a sandbag carried each rope to the ground. The operators on the ground would then sit in the web sling, and slip their hands through wrist loops that were attached to the sling. These would tighten up to prevent the operator from falling; as the helicopter hoisted them up several hundred feet vertically to clear all obstacles on the ground before transiting. The three men would lock arms to prevent oscillation and prevent falls if a rope were shot through; a wounded or unconscious man could fall from the harness unless secured. The system didn't permit the extracted soldiers to be hoisted into the helicopter. They were flown out of the danger area, and then set down in a clearing to board the helicopter.

Soldiers in a McGuire Rig in South Vietnam, 1969.

While effective, the main limitations with the McGuire rig were that it had to be fitted while standing upright, and that the operator's hands were not free to untangle

133

themselves, fire a weapon, or use a radio. Moreover, it was not the capability of choice for extracting wounded or injured personnel. The rig was also uncomfortable and impaired blood circulation. For such reasons, the capability was used only in dire emergency situations that involved short distances of flight.

## STABO Harness

A much improved direct descendant of the McGuire rig, the stabilized body (STABO) extraction capability was first demonstrated in October 1968. It was designed and developed by U.S. Army Special Forces rigger personnel stationed at a RECONDO School established at Nha Trang during the Vietnam War. The capability became widely used, and was quickly adopted by U.S. Navy SEALs and other special units. Like the McGuire rig, the STABO harness was designed to allow military personnel to be rescued by helicopters from jungle or mountain locations where helicopters were unable to land. (Note: RECONDO is an Army acronym for reconnaissance and commando.)

The STABO harness was a machine-stitched body harness, made of heavy-duty nylon webbing identical to that used in parachutes. This harness provided two functions. It was foremost an extraction harness, but it also served, like the Army's standard "H-Gear" (suspenders and a web belt,) to support load-bearing equipment. Later versions of the STABO harness were made in small, medium and large sizes. The main lift harness straps formed an "X" across the operators back. The STABO's leg straps were rolled up and secured with elastic bands to prevent them from dangling loose while patrolling. They would be buckled to

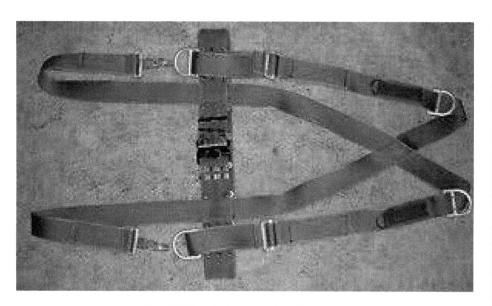

The STABO technical manual and harness.

the harness when the operator was ready to be extracted. The STABO harness could be used to extract a man that was unconscious, and if not unconscious, would allow the operator to remain hands free and still fire his weapon or use a radio.

## Special Purpose Insertion-Extraction System (SPIE)

Pronounced "spy," the Special Purpose Insertion-Extraction (SPIE) capability is the modern-day method of extracting SEALs from places where helicopters cannot land—mountains, jungles, building tops, etc. The capability is practiced often, but is seldom used tactically unless under extreme circumstances. The noise made by the helicopters and the amount of sand, dirt, and rocks that result from the helo's downward rotor wash make it impractical as well as not stealthy.

Navy SEALs suspended from a HH-60H helicopter for a SPIE training operation.

The SPIE system was developed by the Marine Corps 1st Force Reconnaissance Company in the early 1970s as a means to rapidly insert and/or extract a reconnaissance patrol from an area that doesn't permit a helicopter to land. The SPIE system is a much improved adaptation of the Vietnam War-era McGuire and STABO rigs. The SPIE harness, like the STABO, is akin to sitting in a parachute harness. Also, like the STABO, the men are free to use their hands for shooting.

## Rubber Duck Insertion Capability

"Rubber Duck" is a general term applied by Navy SEALs to an aircraft capability where SEAL operators can be transported to an insertion point with a fully or partially inflated combat-equipped Zodiac F-470 Combat Rubber Raiding Craft (CRRC). The capability requires a helicopter with a tail ramp, which might include the U.S. Navy's CH-46 "Sea Knight" and CH-53 "Sea Stallion," Army Special Operation Command's CH-47 "Chinook," and Air Force Special Operations Command's MH-53 "Pave Low" series. The CRRC and SEALs are transported together. At the launch phase, the helicopter hovers just above the water, and the CRRC is pushed out and quickly followed by the SEALs. Once in the water, they climb aboard, prepare the boat for transit, and proceed to the target objective.

U.S. Navy SEALs being lifted by a U.S. Air Force CV-22 tilt-rotor aircraft.

A "Soft-Duck Drop" is the same operation, except it involves deployment of a partially inflated CRRC; to allow the boat to fit in a smaller airframe of a helicopter. Again, the CRRC is pushed out of the helicopter, while it is hovering just above the water at a slow speed, and the SEALs immediately follow the boat into the water, where it is fully inflated to begin the mission.

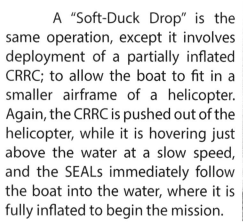

A U.S. Navy CH-46 Sea Knight helicopter with two U.S. Navy SEAL operators.

Artist conception of a CV-22 tilt-rotor aircraft supporting a Rubber Duck operation.

The term "Kangaroo Duck" or "K-Duck" is the term applied to a helicopter insertion capability where SEALs are transported to their insertion point with a fully inflated and mission-loaded CRRC tightly secured to the belly of the helicopter by a D-ring. Like a mother kangaroo with her baby, the CRRC is tucked into the belly of the helicopter during the transit phase of the operation, hence, "Kangaroo Duck" or "K-Duck" for short. The CRRC is released just above the water at the time designated for the launch phase, and quickly followed by the SEALs into the water for the insertion phase.

# CHAPTER 15

# SPECIAL ATOMIC DEMOLITION MUNITION

The Special Atomic Demolition Munition (SADM) was a family of man-portable nuclear weapons fielded by the U.S. military in the 1960s but, fortunately, were never used. Because of tensions between the U.S. and Soviet Union, the contingency plan was to use tactical nuclear weapons primarily in Europe in the event of a Soviet invasion.

The concept was that U.S. Army or Marine Corps personnel could use the weapon to destroy power plants, bridges, dams, and similarly designated targets. It was also intended that the SADM be used against targets in coastal and near-coastal locations, thus, it was and remains a little know fact that the SADM had an underwater and backpack configuration that could be deployed by SEALs and the frogmen of the UDTs. The weapon for use by the UDT-SEAL Teams was designated the B-54 SADM.

UDT-SEAL operator seen in freefall with B-54 SADM trainer.

In theory, the SADM could be delivered by submarines carrying SEAL Delivery Vehicles (SDVs) or by parachute. In training, UDT-SEAL operators, each wearing an underwater breathing apparatus, would be parachuted from an aircraft with the weapon (or delivered by SDV), and swim the device into a harbor or other strategic location. Another UDT-SEAL operator without a SADM would parachute simultaneously to comply with the standing "two-man rule," and to provide support as needed. Air Force regulations require two men to prevent accidental or malicious launch of nuclear weapons by a single individual. The two-man team would emplace the weapon at the designated target location, arm the timer, and swim or ride the SDV back to sea, where they would be retrieved by a submarine or surface support craft.

The UDT and SEAL men quickly realized that any SADM mission would, without doubt, be a suicide mission, since the urgency of the mission would likely require an immediate response, and because they knew they couldn't swim fast enough or far enough to exceed the anticipated blast area. Yet the men accepted this capability as a matter of duty.

Only selected personnel in the UDT and SEAL Teams were trained

A UDT-SEAL operator has released a B-54 SADM trainer in preparation for a water landing.

A B-54 SADM trainer is recovered aboard a support craft after being employed during a UDT-SEAL training exercise.

to prepare and employ the SADM. Because of the rigors of the rules and regulations surrounding nuclear weapons, and the "no fail" nuclear weapons training inspections, it was not a popular capability to maintain. SADM training weapons had to be treated exactly like actual weapons, and failure during Nuclear Weapons Proficiency Inspections could cost several in the chain of command their careers. The SADM was removed from the U.S. military inventory in the 1970s as a result of the Strategic Arms Limitation Talks between the U.S. and the Soviet Union.

# CHAPTER 16

# COMBAT SWIMMERS AND ASTRONAUTS

I was the Executive Officer of Underwater Demolition Team TWENTY-ONE (UDT-21) at the Naval Amphibious Base, Little Creek in Norfolk, Virginia in 1958, which was a component of Underwater Demolition Unit TWO (UDU-2). Over the next two years, Navy frogmen from our command supported the NASA spaceflight program in two separate, but related, long forgotten, undocumented events. The details of both are based on my

Frogmen were involved in the space program from its earliest days. Here a frogman stabilizes the Gemini 3 capsule as John Young and Gus Grissom wait to be picked up by a helicopter to the nearby aircraft carrier, the *USS Intrepid*.

recollections, and in the case of the first event, the shared accounts of retired SEAL operators BMCM Bill Bruhmuller, JO3 Wesley E. Tucker, EMCM Frank Moncrief, and DMCM Lenny Waugh, each of whom were test subjects. Bill provided me a detailed account of his own experience. Wes provided me background material titled "50 Years of Research on Man in Flight" that he obtained from the Air Force Aerospace Medical Research Laboratory, Wright-Patterson AFB, Ohio. Lenny sat for an extended interview. These two events took place several years before the first Mercury splashdown, and before the notoriety that was subsequently experienced by UDT for their at-sea recovery operations in support of Project's Mercury, Gemini, and Apollo.

Like most activities conducted by the UDTs between the wars, they went unnoticed and unrecognized. There were several reasons for this, but the best explanation I can come up with is that our UDTs didn't fit cleanly in the blue water Navy, thus, no one in the hierarchy cared. Moreover, in those days, the men in the UDTs didn't view their service as being extraordinary, and felt no need to talk about it. And probably more important, those of us in leadership positions were very poor at documenting experiences, such as the two I am going to relate.

In the early 1950s, NASA was tasked with exploring the feasibility of space travel. The purpose of Project Mercury was to realize the vision that a human pilot, transported in a life support system (capsule), could be thrust into orbit by a liquid fuel rocket, remain there for several revolutions of the earth, and be safely recovered from orbit. The Air Force had been keenly aware of the need for clarification of the parameters of human endurance, safety, and comfort during periods of unusual stress, and began directing biomedical research toward the development of tests to assist in selecting pilots for special research projects.

# PROJECT MERCURY

## TEST SUBJECT DETACHMENTS

### Wright-Patterson 1958

| Group I | Group II | Group III |
|---|---|---|
| GM1 Thomas McAllister | MMC Robert Sheehan | BM1 Rudolph Boesch |
| SK2 Harvey Collins | EN2 John Lyons | BM1 Fred Robbins |
| DM2 Leonard Waugh | BM3 Louis Kucinski | EN1 Jake Rhinebolt |
| CS3 William Bruhmuller | JO3 Wesley Tucker | SN Ron Gerringer |

Over a four-year period, a series of physiological, psychological, and biochemical evaluations were incorporated into a stress-test program, during which time, several special groups were put through physical and psychological trials, including USAF pilots and young volunteers from the University of Dayton. As time went on, Captain (Medical Corps) Charles L. Wilson, USAF, the principal investigator, came to appreciate that physical fitness, along with the ability to withstand physiological and psychological stress, would play a key factor in the astronaut selection program for Project Mercury. They were having problems establishing standards, because so many people were failing the tests. The word went out to canvas the U.S. military to find the most physically fit men possible, men who didn't get claustrophobic, and men who could withstand extreme stress. That led them to the UDT-21 doorstep in Norfolk, Virginia in the spring of 1958.

The day I got the call, I asked for volunteers. Many put up their hands, but only 12 were chosen. Since four decades have passed, it is not clear what our specific selection criteria was; however, physical fitness and diving experience, particularly under difficult and hazardous conditions, was certainly of prime consideration. The men were divided into three test groups, each with four UDT operators.

## Wright-Patterson Astronaut Physical Fitness Testing

Bill Bruhmuller was in Group 1 and remembers: "I was 20 years old. From a volunteer standpoint, we volunteered for whatever the command asked. You didn't ask a lot of questions and you didn't hesitate. In this case, we didn't know what this thing was about, but we thought, 'what the hell,' and put up our hands. We were always quick to volunteer for any adventure.

"I don't know how we were chosen. It was just certain guys called into the office. We didn't know what was required or how we qualified. Three groups of four were selected for testing at Wright-Patterson Air Force Base in Dayton, Ohio.

"We were not told anything more than that. They said: 'You'll find out when you get there.' All we really knew was that it was something to do with

UDT operator CS3 Bill Bruhmuller was in UDT Group I for testing at Wright-Patterson Air Force Base.

astronauts and in those days, we hardly knew what that was. That word was not much used in the late 1950s. We hadn't even thought of the idea of spacecraft."

When the men arrived at Wright-Patterson, they were put in a remote area of the base. The test facilities were cordoned off so that no one had access to them. The men were put in very basic, regular Air Force barracks, with a chow hall not far away. They were told they would be putting in 14-hour days and the people organizing the testing wanted no distractions. The UDT men were given a few minutes to get settled and told to report for a briefing.

UDT Test Group 1 (l-r): Tom McAllister, Lenny Waugh, Bill Bruhmuller, and Harvey "Rip" Collins. (Courtesy The National Navy SEAL-UDT Museum)

Bill Bruhmuller recounted entering a small, non-descript briefing room where the men were given a short talk about the purpose of the program: "A medical doctor with a German accent told us they were intent on finding out what the human body could physically endure. They were going to send men to do things no one had ever done before. We were to start each day at six in the morning and would work straight through, with meals brought to us. Our days were to be filled with physical and logic tests and a combination of both."

The briefing included an overview of the various tests the UDT volunteers would undertake to study their physical fitness, stamina, motivation and physiological responses. The goal was to establish the standards for selecting the first group of astronauts that would be put through the Special Crew Selection Program. The men were told they we were restricted, not just to the base, but to the barracks area specifically.

The UDT men totally smashed all the records. They did things that the doctors couldn't believe. They were going into the centrifuge and calling for more Gs. Up in an altitude chamber in 133 degree heat they were playing cards—even cheating at cards. Some of the tests they were subjected to included:

**Treadmill and Harvard Step Test** – This test provided a good indication of fitness and ability to recover after a strenuous exercise. It was quickly determined that the level of fitness of UDT personnel was far above average.

**Blood Tests** – They were administered on a regular basis to measure oxygen in the blood, among other things; including stress hormones.

**Flack Test** – It crudely represented motivation, and consisted of blowing into a rubber mouthpiece in such a manner to support a column of mercury at 40 mm for as long as possible. Again, the UDT men exceeded the norm.

**Cold Pressure Test** - This tested motivation along with changes in blood pressure, heart rate, and pulse excitability. Three resting blood pressures and pulses were taken at 1-minute intervals while the subject was relaxed, then he was directed to plunge both feet into a pan of ice water for 7-minutes. Something like diving in the Arctic and Antarctic. Lack of motivation did not seem to be a problem for our folks; pulse excitability was recorded as very low for the UDT men.

**Heat Test** – Each subject was exposed to an ambient temperature of 130 degrees Fahrenheit for three hours while wearing a flight suit, long underwear, socks, and flight boots. Thermocouples were attached to the forehead and back of the hand, and EKG leads were affixed to extremities. Body heat storage provided a measure of the heat that a body will store when exposed to extremely hot environments. At the time, it was the most reliable parameter for evaluating the performance of a subject under heat stress. The better the heat dissipation, the less chance for heat stroke, a condition that has a very high mortality rate. Other than some edginess during card games, the UDT men proved to be good heat subjects. This could have been related to the fact that the men spent considerable time in the sun at St. Thomas, USVI.

**Human centrifuge** – Its purpose was to determine human tolerance for normal and emergency space flight trajectories. The ability to pull a G-force of 6-9 was considered acceptable. All the UDT men were pulling 8-11 G's and calling for more.

**Partial Pressure Suit Test** - The procedure involved being de-nitrogenated on 100% oxygen for two hours, while wearing a helmet and facemask. As soon as de-nitrogenating began, the subjects were fitted with the MC-3 partial pressure suit; with extremity EKG leads being applied. Blood and urine samples were drawn before entering the low-pressure (high-altitude) chamber, which was first brought up to 40,000 feet, then 55,000 feet, and finally 65,000 feet, where the test started and continued for 60-minutes. During the final

30-minutes, the men were exposed to a battery of tests designed to measure psychomotor functions. Following successful completion of the high-altitude test, the men were given the opportunity to briefly experience pressure suit protection at 115,000 feet, for which they all received certification. The MC-3, when worn at 65,000 feet for 1-hour, presented definite physiological and psychological stresses, referred to as "graying-out." Fortunately, none of the UDT men ever saw gray. That said, they did cause the chamber crew quite a bit of anxiety, because they kept falling asleep during the chamber runs. Claustrophobia, from wearing the helmet and pressure suit, was obviously not a problem for the men of UDT.

It wasn't always easy to know what was and wasn't a test of some sort. Bill Bruhmuller recalled: "We would not know what each day would hold until that day arrived. They just popped things on us. We had no idea who planned what or how. We were not intimidated or maybe we were too dumb to worry. As frogmen, we always had the attitude that nothing would worry or scare us. Whatever it is, it is just another job. The rigor of

UDT operator BM1 Rudy Boesch was in UDT Group III for testing at Wright-Patterson Air Force Base.

our initial training set the tone. Once you make the Teams, it doesn't stop. It is a way of life and you don't want to let the guy next to you down."

During centrifuge testing, the first man in was Tom McAllister. He was instructed to keep his eyes open and keep the red lights on the left and right of his peripheral vision in sight. He was given a clicker to hold, and when he could no longer see the lights, he was supposed to click the thing. All of the men looked at each other with the understanding that none of them was going to click it.

The machine spun up and spun up. Most people pass out over 4 or 5 Gs, but McAllister kept going. He never clicked, and the centrifuge only stopped when it hit its pre-set automatic shut-off. When the machine stopped, McAllister's eyes were rolled up in the back of his head. He had surpassed 7 Gs before he passed out.

Bill Bruhmuller summarized the incident: "They asked us at the beginning of the test if we were scared. We weren't. In fact, Tom McAllister passed out because he was too relaxed. SEALs are problem-solvers by culture. No one told us what to do to withstand that kind of pressure, but we talked to Tom after his test, and quickly realized you had to anticipate the Gs and wiggle your toes and use your extremities to pressure your blood to your core. Tom was so relaxed and was thinking about not being dizzy. The next time McAllister went into the centrifuge, he was just fine and so were the rest of us."

The scientists told the men not to worry about Tom. "There is not one man in a million who can take more than 7 Gs. We had to shut it off." That was the challenge for the rest of the men. Two of the men later successfully reached 11 Gs.

It is a Navy SEAL thing to try to find out a weakness and then exploit it. Bill Bruhmuller explained that the frogmen sent to Wright-Patterson didn't want anyone to find their weaknesses, if they had any! "We were determined to do whatever it took no matter what it was, and never let the test administrators find our limits."

## Ongoing Engagement with Space Programs

While the 1956 astronaut fitness testing at Wright-Patterson was UDT's first involvement in the spaceflight program, it was not the last. Indeed, U.S. Navy SEALs continued to be involved through the Apollo program, and two SEALs have gone on to become astronauts and participants through deployment to the International Space Station that continues to orbit the earth.

Some months after our men returned from Wright-Patterson, I got a call from one of the candidates that had gone through screening for the Mercury program. I didn't find out until years later that it was Navy Commander Scott Carpenter. Carpenter and the rest of the original astronauts were at Langley Air Force

The Mercury Seven join the men from UDT-21 in the spring of 1959 for diver training. All of the astronauts can be identified from the front row (l-r) The first man is UDT LT Norm Ott, then Wally Schirra, Gordon Cooper, Alan Shepard, John Glenn, (Gus Grissom is behind and between Shepard and Glenn), Scott Carpenter, and Deke Slayton at the far right. (Courtesy of the National Navy SEAL-UDT Museum)

Base in Hampton, Virginia, which was not far from Little Creek, where they were doing some training. He explained he was one of the astronauts, and that they had all heard about us from the program administrators at Wright-Patterson. The legendary ability of our guys to overcome claustrophobia had made an impression on everyone, and they had heard it was because of our guys' diving experience. They wanted SCUBA training. In addition to mastering claustrophobia, they felt that the training would help them deal with weightlessness and could help them if they needed to jettison the space capsule upon splashdown. Furthermore, they were headed to a place called Cape Canaveral, then a little-known and sparsely populated spot on the Florida coast. They thought SCUBA would be a nice form of recreation.

I got this call before the big announcement about the "Mercury Seven" astronauts. Mercury was the name of the spaceflight program, and "Seven" was the number of astronauts selected to participate in the space flights. They were not yet famous and I had only the vaguest idea of what an astronaut was. I said, "Okay," and didn't pay much more attention to it. I arranged them to come over and set up a team to give them two weeks of training.

Four of the Mercury astronauts can be seen going out with UDT men on their dive boat. John Glenn is seated at the center of the picture. Behind him is Gus Grissom. Alan Shepard is at Glenn's left, and Gordon Cooper is at the bottom right of the photo in front of Alan. (Courtesy of the National Navy SEAL-UDT Museum)

Training these guys was a challenge for both sides. Of course, we gave them the same kind of training we got in Basic Underwater Demolition training—not Hell Week exactly, but we didn't go easy on them. Frank Moncrief was one of the instructors: "We'd give them a full tank of air, send them down, and tell them they can't come up for anything. Then we harassed them like they do in BUD/S; ripping their air hoses out, turning off their air valves, stealing their masks or ripping off their fins. It is about problem-solving under stress. They

To assist in astronaut recovery, UDT frogmen jumped from helicopters to attach flotation collars on the returning space capsules to prevent them from sinking. The astronauts would remain in the capsule until the flotation collar was fully secured. Note the green dye that was automatically released after splashdown to make it easier to see the capsule from the air.

Frogmen stabilize the Gemini 3 capsule as pilot John Young waits in a life raft to be picked up by a helicopter along with command pilot Gus Grissom to flown to the nearby aircraft carrier, the *USS Intrepid*.

had to recover from all these little things without panicking and coming to the surface. We did our best to give them a rough time."

The frogmen got along well with those original seven astronauts. Those guys had to be tough, because each had achieved or exceeded the standards at Wright-Patterson that our guys helped establish. They were hot-shot pilots and were a great deal of fun to be with. We fit in well with them and they fit in well with us, with respect on both sides. We didn't look at them as anything special beyond that. The media hype came later.

When the training was over, the astronauts had a party over at Langley for their UDT instructors. It was a raucous party at the officer's club, and we all had a very good time.

A team of frogmen led by LTjg Chris Bent secure flotation to the Gemini 6 capsule.

Years later, I was giving a keynote speech at a symposium at the Naval Academy. Scott Carpenter was at the session and heard me tell the story of the astronauts getting SCUBA training. After the talk, he found me in the crowd and said, "You didn't know who called? I am the guy."

In was in the early 1950s when NASA decided to utilize water landings for spacecraft and crews returning from their flights. The fledgling space agency relied heavily on the UDTs to help establish an effective astronaut survival and recovery program. At the request of NASA in May 1961, UDT personnel began training the "Mercury Seven" astronaut corps how to safely egress their capsule after it splashed down in the ocean.

Initially, the Navy didn't plan to have the UDTs participate in the actual recoveries. However, after a successful splashdown of America's second manned space flight in July 1961, the spacecraft sank and astronaut Gus Grissom nearly drowned. With the sinking of Grissom's Mercury capsule *Liberty Bell 7*, the use of swimmers to install flotation collars on Gemini and Apollo capsules became NASA policy. Before the loss of Grissom's capsule, NASA had chosen water landings as opposed to the "terra firma" landings by the Russians. Combat swimmers from the Navy's UDTs on both coasts were assigned to be the men in the water at splashdown. Navy frogmen assisted in the recovery at splashdown of nine Gemini and Apollo spacecraft and their on-board astronauts.

LTjg Chris Bent is seen jumping from an SH-53 Sea King helicopter to assist in the recovery of the Gemini 6 spacecraft. The men of UDT-21 can be seen attaching a flotation collar to stabilize the capsule and provide safety during astronaut egress. This was mission AS-201, and represented the first recovery of an Apollo spacecraft, which took place near the Ascension Islands. The mission involved a suborbital unmanned flight by astronauts Tom Stafford and Wally Schirra. The primary recovery team included LTjg Chris Bent, Dan Fraser, and Roger Bates. The backup team was Ensign Bill White, Joe Gay, and "P.T." Smith.

LTjg Chris Bent is seen in an Emerson closed-circuit, pure oxygen rebreather, which was UDT's tactical diving apparatus. It was not used for spaceflight recoveries.

Frogmen assemble collars around space capsules and then use C02 cylinders to inflate them to stabilize the capsules and keep them from sinking.

Gemini 7 recovery December 18 1965: LTJjg Chris Bent is behind astronauts Frank Bormann and Jim Lovell. UDT operator Dan Fraser is assisting on the raft; David Sutherland is in water.

Astronaut Jim Lovell is being hoisted from the recovery raft into a U.S Navy SH-53 helicopter for return to the host aircraft carrier *USS Wasp (CVS-18)*. Astronaut Frank Bormann will also be taken aboard the support helicopter.

Astronauts Neil Armstrong and David R. Scott sit with their spacecraft hatches open while awaiting arrival of the recovery ship, the *USS Leonard F. Mason (DD-852)*, after successful completion of their *Gemini 8* mission. They're assisted by UDT personnel. The overhead view shows the Gemini 8 spacecraft with the yellow flotation collar attached to stabilize the spacecraft in choppy seas.

NASA prepared a training manual, which was used in conjunction with a boilerplate mock-up of Gemini and Apollo Spacecraft. Team members were assigned for the upcoming missions; NASA provided classroom training, and in-the water drills until the installation of the flotation collar could be accomplished safely, quickly, and efficiently. These evolutions took place at the Naval Amphibious Base, Little Creek, Virginia. Mercury, Gemini, and early Apollo flights splashed down in the Atlantic; the manned Apollo flights for lunar missions re-entered over the Pacific. Some of the surviving training modules can be seen at the National Navy UDT SEAL Museum in Fort Pierce, Florida.

Apollo capsule recovery operations.

Frogman Clancey Hatleberg greets the first men to walk on the moon from the Apollo 11 command capsule. The recovery team members also included Wes Chesser, Mike Mallory, and John Wolfram. They can be seen wearing Biological Isolation Garments (BIG suits), because NASA was concerned about contamination by lunar microbes. (Photo Courtesy Mike Mallory)

In this picture, frogman Clancy Hatleberg removes his BIG suit following the successful recovery of the astronauts.

The team battled 10-foot-high waves and 28-mph winds to attach a 200-pound inflatable flotation ring around the Apollo 11 capsule. Frogman Mike Mallory snapped this picture of teammates Wes Chesser and John Wolfram after the successful operation to recover the command capsule from Apollo 11. (Photo Courtesy Mike Mallory)

Gemini 6 Astronauts James McDivitt and Edward White are met by UDT frogmen after they have secured the vessel with a flotation collar.

Navy frogman LTjg Chris Bent outside the Apollo capsule prior to opening the hatch.

The UDT swimmers wore complete neoprene wet suits and donned full SCUBA gear for the recovery and collar installation. Nitrogen tetroxide was the propellant that fueled the attitude re-entry nozzles in the small end of the spacecraft and, if this fuel leaked, NASA wanted the swimmers to use SCUBA in case of possibly contaminated air. SCUBA also facilitated installation of the flotation collar. This horseshoe shaped device went around the capsule and with webbing hooked up side to side making a sling to support the spacecraft. After it was assembled, the swimmers used either of two $CO_2$ cylinders to inflate the "collar."

Once the collar was inflated, the swimmers plugged in a hand-held phone and assured the astronauts that the hatches could be opened. This flotation system would support the Gemini and Apollo vehicles, even

# RECOVERING FIRST MEN TO WALK ON THE MOON
## FROGMAN MIKE MALLORY REMEMBERS

### Apollo 11 - July 24, 1969

I was the only guy in the water with a camera—actually a bunch of cameras. The reporters from the photo pool handed me one of theirs. NASA and the Navy each gave me cameras. I also had some of my own. These were pretty fancy outfits for the time—waterproof Nikons.

I had to jump from the helicopter, swim to the capsule, secure the flotation collar, help out the astronauts, then return to the ship with them and climb and 80 foot ladder up—all with these many cameras. I did give one to the helicopter crew so they could get a few pictures from their perspective, too.

It was a rough day, but as a SEAL, we were trained for ocean swimming, locking out of submarines in the dark, hitting enemy beaches like I did in Vietnam. The news reports from that day talked about the rough seas and 10 foot high waves and near gale force winds, but it was like a vacation for us—easy day. The capsule was tossed around quite a bit. Neil Armstrong and Buzz Aldrin, after being weightless for so long, were a bit woozy from being put through the ocean tumble cycle. They were pretty glad to see us.

When I got down to the ship's dark room with the reporters and photojournalists to start developing my film, they all gathered around to see my negatives. They had huge telephoto lenses trained on us during recovery, but when they saw what I had, they said: "We're going with froggy's pictures."

if the capsules flooded with the astronauts on board, which never happened. The astronauts were required to inflate their Life Preserver Units once the hatches were opened. This assured flotation if they became immersed. The astronauts were usually hoisted up to the helicopter; however, on two occasions they remained inside the spacecraft, and were hoisted directly aboard the aircraft carrier.

For the Gemini recoveries, a Navy task force was deployed for each mission. It included an aircraft carrier, helicopters, the UDT swimmers, NASA officials, and the media. The ship deployed early enough to allow training and rehearsals. A boiler plate mock-up was put in the water then a simulation of splash-down took place. Rehearsals were held in daylight and darkness; because, although the scheduled splashdowns were planned for day light, an emergency descent could have occurred at night.

During actual missions and moments after re-entry, drogue parachutes in the Earth Landing System were deployed at an altitude of about 10,000 feet by a barometric switch. They would slow the descent down to roughly 124 mph, and would be programmed to be cut away. At the same time, pilot parachutes pulled three large main parachutes from their containers; slowing the spacecraft to about 22 mph for splashdown, where the parachutes would be released. A radio beacon began transmitting, and a dye marker was dispersed to facilitate spotting from the air. Splashdown occurred as far as 92 miles away from the recovery ship and as close as half a mile.

Once the re-entering spacecraft was picked up on radar, two teams of recovery swimmers, primary and backup, boarded two SH-53 Sea King helicopters with the collars and a life raft. Often the helicopters in vicinity of the anticipated splashdown could spot the Gemini suspended below its deployed orange and white chutes, and observe its descent and splashdown.

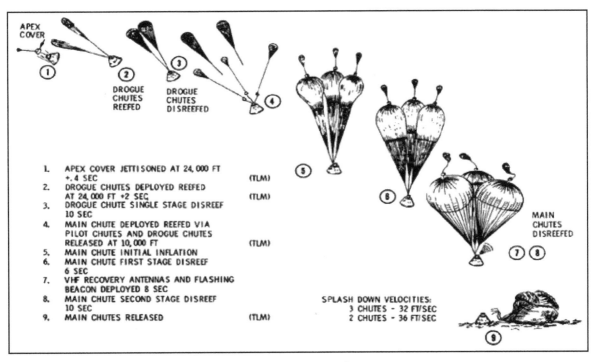

Earth Landing System sequence of events.

The designated helicopter approached the floating spacecraft into the wind. Making a slow pass alongside the capsule at about 18 feet above the water the first swimmer exited, then the second, then the collar and raft were pushed out by the last swimmer and helicopter crewman and then the last swimmer jumped into the water. The swimmers installed the flotation collar, activated the C02 inflation system, then connected the phone they carried and told the astronauts they could open the hatches. A raft was then inflated and made fast to the collar to facilitate egress of the astronauts if they chose to return to the recovery ship by helicopter. Within an hour or two, the carrier came alongside, the spacecraft was hoisted aboard, and the UDT swimmers were recovered. Mission complete.

These recovery procedures were continually refined and well documented by the start of the Apollo program. The initial lunar landing mission of Apollo 11, however, presented a significant additional challenge. The world's health and science community was worried about returning missions carrying lunar pathogens that could harm human, plant, or animal life. The frogmen were required to wear Biological Isolation Garments (BIG Suits) as a precaution.

On July 23 at 0550 *USS Hornet* time, the Apollo 11 Command Module *Columbia* landed in the Pacific Ocean about 920 miles southwest of Pearl Harbor, and immediately turned upside-down as a result of wave and wind action. Within the seven minutes required for the spacecraft's righting system to successfully turn it upright, the UDT men arrived and took control of the operation. After all necessary preparations were accomplished, the hatch was opened and the astronauts exited into the decontamination raft. The UDT men continued with their task of preparing *Columbia* and its cargo of Moon rocks for retrieval by the ship's crane.

All of this was, of course, being broadcast around the world; thus, it is almost certain that no other UDT or SEAL operation has ever been conducted before such a huge audience—an estimated 500 million people watched the recovery operation live on TV in many countries around the world.

Captain William "Bill" Shepherd became the first Navy SEAL in space when he was selected to become a NASA astronaut in 1989.

## Frogmen in Space

SEALs are headed higher still. A new generation of frogmen are not content just to take to the skies or play a supporting role in NASA. They are blasting into space.

In the Space Shuttle era, splashdowns became a thing of the past, however, frogmen continued to play a role, when Captain William Shepherd became the first SEAL astronaut. His SEAL career began when he applied for Basic Underwater Demolition/SEAL training (BUD/S) in 1972 after graduating from the United States Naval Academy the prior year. He served with the Underwater Demolition Team ELEVEN, SEAL Teams ONE and TWO, and Special Boat Unit TWENTY.

In 1993, Bill Shepherd was assigned as the first commander of the International Space Station (ISS). From October 31, 2000 to March 21, 2001, he and Russian cosmonauts Yuri Gidzenko and Sergey Krikalev became the first crew of *Expedition 1*. SEAL Astronaut Bill Shepherd logged over 159 days in space. Bill achieved the rank of Captain in the U.S. Navy.

Seeking even greater challenges, Captain Shepherd applied unsuccessfully for NASA Astronaut Group 9 in 1980. With a typical SEAL no-quit attitude, applied again and became the first military non-aviator selected by NASA four years later. Tragically, his SEAL training was put to use following the crash of the Space Shuttle Challenger, when he joined other Navy divers in the salvage operation.

Captain Shepherd went on to serve on three Space Shuttle flights as a Mission Specialist in 1988, 1990, and 1992.

The next year, he became Program Manager of the International Space Station. Political delays in Russia, and cost issues, delayed the mission for a number of years. It wasn't until 31 October 2000 that he, as

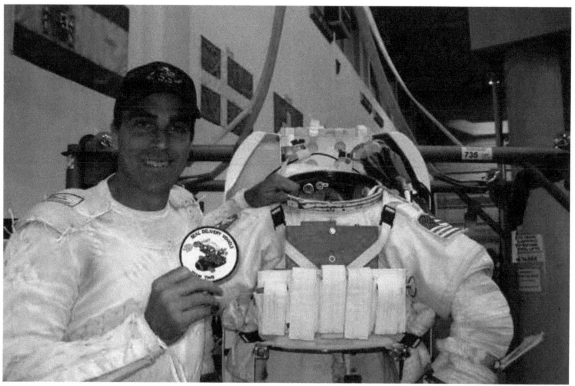

During *Expedition 35*, Captain Cassidy and European Space Agency astronaut Luca Parmitano made an unplanned spacewalk to replace a pump controller box. The excursion was cut short when Parmitano had cooling water leak into his helmet.

Mission Commander, and Russian cosmonauts Yuri Gidzenko and Sergey Krikalev, launched into space on Expedition 1, to serve as the first crew of the station.

Captain Shepherd returned to earth for the final time on March 21, 2001. He then returned to the Navy; finishing his active duty career on the staff of Commander, Naval Special Warfare Command, where he helped develop new capabilities and programs for the SEAL and Special Boat programs until he retired in 2002.

Captain Christopher John "Chris" Cassidy, followed in Captain Shepherd's footsteps. After graduating from the United States Naval Academy in 1993, and completing training with BUD/S Class 192 in 1994 as class honor man, he served two deployments to Afghanistan, one just weeks after the September 11 attacks, during which he earned a Bronze Star with a combat V. He went on to earn a Master's degree in ocean engineering from MIT in 2000.

After 10 years in the SEAL Teams, and while serving as Platoon Commander at SEAL Delivery Vehicle Team TWO in Norfolk, he applied to become an astronaut. He was selected in 2004, and completed Astronaut Candidate Training in 2006. He served as a Mission Specialist on Space Shuttle Endeavor for mission STS-127 in 2009, and joined the Expedition 35 crew in 2013; serving as flight engineer. It was on this flight that he became the 500th man in space.

The most recent Navy SEAL astronaut candidate, Lieutenant Doctor Jonny Kim, was selected by NASA on June 7, 2017.

As of this writing, Captain Cassidy remains on active duty, and serves as Chief of the Astronaut Office at NASA, where he is responsible for flight assignments, mission preparation, on orbit support of U.S. crews, and organizing astronaut office support.

The men of UDTs Atlantic and Pacific established a proud tradition with their participation in America's manned spaceflight program throughout the 1960's. NASA's Constellation Program envisions returning to the Moon about 2020, and may once again use water landings upon return to earth. It is certainly possible that U.S. Navy SEALs will again be called upon to support our manned space-exploration programs.

Indeed, on June 7, 2017, NASA announced the members of the 2017 astronaut class. From over 18,300 applicants, NASA chose 12 women and men as the agency's new astronaut candidates. Among them was Navy SEAL Lieutenant Dr. Jonny Kim. NASA announced this class will be training for "deep space" missions. Jonny started astronaut training in August of 2017 for a two year process that will ultimately send another Navy SEAL into space.

SEALs are clearly becoming comfortable operating in the sea, air, land—and beyond.

# ABOUT THE AUTHOR

Captain Olson is a graduate of the U.S. Merchant Marine Academy. Following graduation, he sailed as a ship's officer in the Merchant Marine and U.S. Navy. In 1955, he volunteered for Underwater Demolition Team (UDT) Replacement Training (now Basic Underwater Demolition/SEAL, known as BUD/S), graduating in East Coast Class 15 at the Little Creek Naval Amphibious Base in Norfolk, Virginia.

Six months later, while assigned to UDT-21, he was designated as Officer-in-Charge to lead the first detachment of 15 frogmen to attend the U.S. Army's Basic Airborne and Jumpmaster Course at Fort Benning, Georgia.

In the 1950s and early 1960s, there were no career opportunities for officers that aspired to a career in the UDT-SEAL community. Virtually every junior officer was classified as a reservist serving on active duty. As a result, they would normally leave the Navy after a single tour of duty. In late December 1959, after serving in UDT-21 for four years, with the last 18 months as executive officer, Lieutenant Olson left the Team and returned to civilian life. During his tenure at UDT-21, he had validated the requirement for a water-entry technique by parachute. His work in this area resulted in Army Airborne Training becoming a requirement for all frogmen and subsequently SEALs.

After a period of reflection, Norm decided to capitalize on his professional training and shipboard experience as a Mariner, and returned to active duty by going to sea. He was assigned as Chief Engineer in the flagship of the Atlantic Fleet Amphibious Force. During this tour, he was promoted to Lieutenant Commander and augmented into the regular Navy (i.e., a designated career officer vs. a reserve officer).

In the early 1960s, unconventional warfare clouds were looming in Vietnam, and there was a scarcity of middle-grade officers with the knowledge, know-how and experience to fill this need. Fortuitously, Lieutenant Commander Olson had the professional reputation, credentials, and availability to be selected as the Commanding Officer of UDT-11. Over a three-year period, his command conducted classified combat operations in the coastal regions of South Vietnam; including the training of counterpart allies throughout Southeast Asia. Concurrently, he formed and led what subsequently became the U.S. Navy Parachute Demonstration Team—"Leap Frogs."

In 1967 and 68, he was assigned to the U.S. Military Assistance Command, Vietnam - Studies and Observation Group (USMACV-SOG) as Commanding Officer, U.S. Naval Advisory Detachment (USNAD) Vietnam, with the responsibility for planning and executing clandestine and covert maritime special operations. Additionally, he maintained his parachute skills by logging 17 tactical training jumps from various SOG aircraft. On his last jump, he was accompanied by SOC's Commander, Colonel "Jack" Singlaub, a retired two-star general, who later served as National Director and Chairman of the Board of the Parachute Club of America, forerunner of the United States Parachute Association.

Upon returning from Vietnam, Commander Olson was assigned to Naval Special Warfare Group ATLANTIC in Norfolk, Virginia, where he formed and led the UDT-SEAL Para-Team (East). The team subsequently adopted the name "Chuting Stars," which was the name of the original U.S. Navy Parachute Demonstration Team, which no longer existed.

In mid-1970, he attended the Naval War College as a student and then served on the Pentagon staff. He was deep selected for Captain and transferred to the Naval Inshore Warfare Command, ATLANTIC staff as Assistant Chief of Staff, Operations/Plans. From there, he was assigned as Commanding Officer, Naval Amphibious Base, Little Creek, Norfolk, Virginia, and finally as Commodore, Naval Special Warfare Group, TWO, also at Little Creek. He served his final three-year tour in the Navy as the first Chief of Staff of the newly formed Joint Special Operations Command, Fort Bragg, North Carolina.

Having been instrumental in establishing and leading the early Leap Frogs and Chuting Stars, and being intimately involved with the aforementioned parachute-related commands, he continued to achieve and hone his parachuting skills as a life-long member of the U.S. Parachute Association (#307). He held License C-1998 and D-1062; Diamond Freefall Wings #101 (24- hours freefall time); Ratings as Jumpmaster, Rigger, and Instructor; and qualifications in the military airbornes of Greece, South Vietnam, Thailand, and Germany.

In 1983, Captain Olson retired from the U.S. Navy with over 30 years' commissioned service, spanning the Korean Police Action, Vietnam Conflict, and Cold War. He excelled at every level throughout his Navy SEAL career, gaining respect for his operational skills, logical approach to problem solving, and no-nonsense leadership.

Following retirement from the Navy, Captain Olson worked in the private sector for 16 years; initially as Director of Security for the Reagan-Bush '84 Authorized Campaign Committee, and, after that, as Founding Director of the National Navy UDT-SEAL Museum (now Director Emeritus). He later served as Director of Industrial Security for the Electric Boat Division of General Dynamics Corporation, and fully retired after a stint as General Manager in support of Small Business Innovative Research Programs at the Navy Research Laboratory in Panama City, Florida, and the Systems Engineering and Technical Assistance contract at the U.S. Special Operations Command (USSOCOM) in Tampa, Florida.

In 2005, at age 74, with 2,200 jumps in his log book, Captain Olson fulfilled the last phase of his parachuting career. At the end of a six-year period, he made his 4,000th freefall jump on March 14, 2011, his 80th birthday. Under clear skies at Skydive City, he participated in a clean 30-way formation that was

In 2002, Captain Norm Olson was the recipient of the U.S. Special Operations Command Medal for a lifetime of contributing to Naval Special Warfare and US Special Operations. His award was presented by Admiral (SEAL) Eric Olson and Naval Special Warfare Command Force Master Chief (SEAL) Rick Rogers. Nine years later, Captain Olson was inducted into the U.S. Special Operation Command "Commando Hall of Honor."

Polo Shirt worn in honor of the original Navy Parachute Demonstration Team - Chuting Stars (1961- 1971).

Captain Olson's 4000th jump at Skydive City, Zephyrhills, Florida, on his 80th birthday from two jump-configured Twin Otter aircraft. He is located at 6 o'clock in Viagra blue.

completed at 9,000 feet. Additionally, Captain Olson was recognized for attaining 60-hours in freefall, and being inducted into the Jumpers Over Eighty Society (JOES). At the drop zone, he was irreverently referred to as the "Sky Fossil!"

# SKYDIVING IS A VERY CIVILIZED SPORT

Skydiving is a very civilized sport, the most civilized. It is proper that it came from France, the land of rationality. The mark of civilization is the use of reason to control emotion. When you jump, you have to use your mind to overcome panic and fear, and when you're more proficient, carelessness and laziness. It's a very private thing – something you do for its own sake. Once you get out of that plane, you feel safe and free.

These words were spoken in 1961 by Samuel H Beer, a fifty-five year old grandfather and a professor at Harvard University. He began jumping out of curiosity and found himself fascinated.

80 Years Loving Life!
Happy Birthday!
2011

GEORGE BUSH

September 2, 2016

Dear Norman,

Lisa Merriam sent me the nicest letter about you and the extraordinary feat you accomplished in establishing the National Navy SEAL Museum, and I write simply to say, WELL DONE! I "viewed" the Museum online and was mighty impressed. Again I say, WELL DONE; and I wish you continued success with the Museum and with your upcoming book.

This fellow Navy man and former Commander-in-Chief salutes you and all SEALsb, current and former, for your heroic service to our country. You are, indeed, the best America has to offer.

With respect and warmest regards,

Captain Norman Olson, USN (Ret)
1933 Cordero Court
The Villages, FL 32159-8566

In 1944, future President George Bush served as a Navy torpedo bomber pilot in the Pacific theater of World War II. During his 58th combat mission, his plane was set ablaze after he released his bombs before bailing out over the water. After floating on a raft for four hours, he was picked up by the Navy submarine *USS Finback*. His bravery in action earned him the Distinguished Flying Cross, three Air Medals and a Presidential Unit Citation.

Sixty years after he bailed out of a disabled aircraft, the former Commander in Chief made his first freefall skydive at age 80 with the U.S. Army "Golden Knights". Ten years later, he marked his eighth and final skydive on his 90th birthday. He is the Honorary Chairman of the International Skydiving Museum & Hall of Fame.

# USSOCOM COMMANDO
# HALL OF HONOR

After a 21-year layoff from skydiving, Norm Olson adopted Skydive City in Zephyrhills, Forida as his home drop zone for the next six years. It was also the training drop zone of the Special Operations Command Parachute Team "Para-Commandos." As a result of his relationship with the team, he was made an Honorary Para-Commando and was included on selective training jumps.

On the morning before his 4,000 jump, he was invited to make two skydives with the team in the company of Admiral Eric T. Olson, Commander Special Operations Command. Following the two jumps and during the debrief, the Admiral informed Norm that he was going to be inducted into the U.S. Special Operations Command Commando Hall of Honor in May 2011 for having served with distinction within the Special Operations Forces community.

The Hall of Honor was established in 2010 and recognizes those who have served with great distinction and have demonstrated leadership and selfless service within the SOF community. The inductees are listed on the USSOCOM Commando Hall of Honor website: https://www.socom.mil/hall-of-heroes/commando-hall-of-heroes

# INTERNATIONAL SKYDIVING MUSEUM AMBASSADOR

Six years later in September 2017, Colonel Kirk Knight, U.S. Army Retired, a Trustee for the International Skydiving Museum and Hall of Fame invited Norm to be an Ambassador for the Museum, and to join the list of distinguished supporters of the museum and the pioneers of our sport. He gladly accepted, particularly in view of Kirk Knight's own distinguished career as a former Commander of the "Golden Knights" while on active duty, and his current stature as a key member of the USSOCOM "Para-Commandos."

CPSIA information can be obtained
at www.ICGtesting.com
Printed in the USA
LVHW02*0750181117
556740LV00009B/23/P